Doing Cultural Anthropology

Doing Cultural Anthropology

Projects for Ethnographic Data Collection

Michael V. Angrosino

University of South Florida

WAVELAND

PRESS, INC.

Prospect Heights, Illinois

For information about this book, contact:
Waveland Press, Inc.
P.O. Box 400
Prospect Heights, Illinois 60070
(847) 634-0081
www.waveland.com

This book is dedicated
to the memory of Julia G. Crane—
inspiring teacher, generous mentor, and good friend

Contents

Acknowledgments   ix

Introduction   1
Michael V. Angrosino

1 Becoming a Participant Observer   9
Gerry Tierney

2 Exploring Genealogy   19
Constance P. deRoche

3 Conducting a Life History Interview   33
Michael V. Angrosino

4 Analyzing Narrative Data   45
Nancy Redfern-Vance

**5 Reconstructing a Community
through Archival Research**   63
Cheryl Rodriguez & Yvette Baber

 6 **Using a Museum as a Resource for
    Ethnographic Research**   **71**
    Serena Nanda

 7 **Learning about Formal Organizations**   **81**
    V. Richard Persico, Jr.

 8 **Free-Listing Vocabulary**   **91**
    J. Jerome Smith

 9 **Observing a Workplace**   **99**
    Kathryn Borman, Ellen Puccia, Amy Fox McNulty, & Bill Goddard

10 **Carrying Out a Structured Observation**   **107**
    Laurie J. Price

11 **Designing a Questionnaire for
    Cross-Cultural Research**   **115**
    Roberta D. Baer & Susan C. Weller

12 **Working with Numerical Data**   **123**
    Martha W. Rees

13 **Constructing a Virtual Ethnography**   **129**
    S. Elizabeth Bird & Jessica Barber

14 **Developing an Electronic Ethnography**   **139**
    Alvin W. Wolfe & Guy Hagen

15 **Composing Autoethnographic Stories**   **151**
    Leigh Berger & Carolyn Ellis

16 **Participating in an Ethnographic Field School**   **167**
    James M. Tim Wallace

    Contributors 177

Acknowledgments

I am deeply grateful to Thomas Curtin, the Anthropology Editor of Waveland Press, who has been a faithful supporter of *Field Projects in Anthropology* for many years, and whose insightful comments about a possible new edition of that handbook led directly to this new endeavor.

All the contributors to this volume deserve special thanks for responding to my call for chapters in a timely and efficient manner, and for producing such readable and useful essays. I also thank my students at the University of South Florida whose experiences and expressed needs in doing ethnographic research have shaped my approach to the material. I acknowledge the clerical and editorial assistance of Petra LeClair.

Most of all, however, I acknowledge my great debt to Julia Crane, my teacher, mentor, colleague, and friend of more than three decades. Although she was unable to participate directly in the preparation of this book, her approach to the learning of ethnography, her knowledge of and unflagging enthusiasm for field research, and her affection and respect for students shaped my outlook. In a very real sense, this book is her production as much as it mine and the contributors'.

Introduction

Michael V. Angrosino

ETHNOGRAPHY

The English word "ethnography" derives from Greek and literally means the description of a people and its way of life. In contemporary social science, ethnography refers both to a process of research and to the account (usually in writing, but also possibly on film) that results from that research.

The tradition of producing descriptive accounts of the customs and practices of different peoples goes back to classical antiquity—the histories of the Greek Herodotus and the Roman Tacitus are enlivened by such details. Accounts of "exotic" people published by travelers, soldiers, merchants, and missionaries were mainstays of popular literature for many centuries, but it was not until the nineteenth century that attempts were made to systematize the research process that gave rise to these representations of other ways of life. At that point, ethnography became associated with the new discipline of cultural anthropology—indeed, it became the foundation for that new science, concerned as it was with the comparative analysis of the peoples of the world and their cultures. In fact, the greatest insight of cultural anthropology was the concept of culture itself—the idea that people's behaviors, beliefs, interactions, and material productions were not random, but rather formed a "complex whole" that was meaningful, logical, more or less consistent, and worthy of respect on its own terms. And such a concept of culture required the careful and objective collection and analysis of the many details of cultures around the world so as to better understand how those details came together to give substance to culture.

Nineteenth-century ethnographies were originally produced on what is sometimes referred to as a "notes and queries" model. That is, amateur observers (those who, like the travelers and missionaries of previous times, were actively involved with people of different cultures) provided information on demand to scholars seeking to piece together accounts of unfamiliar cultures. For example, Lewis Henry Morgan, one of the founding fathers of anthropology in the United States, constructed a groundbreaking ethnography of kinship systems based on material sent to him by globetrotting nonanthropologists responding to specific questions posed by Morgan at his desk in Rochester, New York. But by the turn of the twentieth century, two models of "direct" ethnography had come into fashion. The first was the systematic ethnographic survey, in which teams of scientists went out to collect as much information as possible about large sections of previously undocumented parts of the world; this approach was modeled on the natural-history surveys of unexplored lands that had been undertaken by nineteenth-century scientists. (Darwin's famous Voyage of the *Beagle*, in the course of which he refined the principles of the theory of evolution, was just such a natural-history survey.) Of greater lasting influence, however, was the intensive study, which usually involved a single researcher living in a single indigenous community for an extended period of time. This approach, typically associated with the pioneering work of Franz Boas in the United States and Bronislaw Malinowski in Britain, has remained the hallmark of cultural anthropology, and has also been adopted and adapted by scholars in the fields of sociology, social psychology, cultural geography, communication, epidemiology, education, and business.

That social scientists representing these diverse disciplines use the ethnographic method demonstrates its value for answering questions about human communities and institutions. Ethnography is distinguished from other ways of conducting social research (e.g., the experimental design) in that it is conducted in "natural" (as opposed to laboratory) settings, in which the behavior of people in everyday situations is followed as it happens—there is no attempt to control any of the variables that might affect that behavior. Ethnographers refer to this natural setting as "the field." The process of doing ethnography is therefore often called "fieldwork." The naturalistic approach implies an inductive analytical strategy; that is, explanatory theories grow out of the experience as it is observed in real life (in contrast to the classic experimental design, in which some general theory generates specific hypotheses, which are then tested under controlled circumstances).

DATA-COLLECTION TECHNIQUES

Ethnography may be thought of as a general strategy for conducting research, the end-product of which is some sort of description of a group and its beliefs, behaviors, and material goods. But ethnography is not, in and of itself, a way to gather information. There are, in fact, many techniques that may be employed to collect data in the course of ethnographic fieldwork. Ethnographers typically use multiple techniques in the field. No data-collection technique is without its limitations and potential biases, so that the more of them that are used, the more chance there is to cancel out those limitations and come up with a reasonably objective overall portrait. Interviewing and observing are the fundamental ethnographic data-collection techniques, but any means of gleaning information that contributes to a description of a people and its way of life can be considered appropriate to ethnographic fieldwork.

THE PHILOSOPHY OF THIS BOOK

In 1974, I was invited by Julia Crane, who had been my dissertation advisor and under whose guidance I had conducted my first fieldwork outside the United States, to co-author a book on ethnographic methods. In those days, there were relatively few courses in ethnographic methods, and most of those in existence were geared to graduate students in anthropology and sociology. We believed, however, that even beginning students in those disciplines could profit from an understanding of ethnography. We agreed that every student, when presented with a body of substantive material such as might be found in the textbooks and lectures associated with introductory survey courses, should ask first of all: "How did s/he come to know this?" In other words, by what process of research did a scholar establish that this or that purported fact or interpretation was worthy of being passed along to those learning about the material?

We nonetheless realized that there was little impact in simply telling students that, for example, Crane learned about 200 years of labor-migration patterns in the Dutch West Indies by an analysis of census records. It would be much better if students were able to experience for themselves what it would be like to work with census records—even if only in the limited context of a small practice exercise—so that they would have a better understanding of and appreciation for what a fieldworker has to go through in order to come up with the material presented so succinctly in a textbook or lecture.

Our book, *Field Projects in Anthropology: A Student Handbook* (1992, Prospect Heights, IL: Waveland Press), therefore took the form of guided exercises in the more prominent data-collection techniques, based on the philosophy of learning-by-doing. The book has gone into three editions, and has been translated into other languages as well. It has proven to be a durable and, we hope, useful tool that has introduced beginning students to the enjoyment of using ethnographic fieldwork as problem solving; it has also been helpful to more advanced students looking to brush up their skills before launching into more elaborate field research projects. The book has been used as a text in formal courses in ethnographic methods (and there are now many more of them—and in disciplines beyond anthropology and sociology—than was the case back in the 1970s) and as supplementary material in introductory surveys. Over the years, the literature on ethnographic data collection has grown enormously, some of it sharing our learn-by-doing philosophy.

It is now time to revisit the material in the *Handbook*. Some of the data-collection techniques that were popular with researchers in the 1960s and 1970s and were therefore featured prominently in that book are no longer quite so common (e.g., componential analysis). Others that seemed somewhat marginal to ethnographers then have become increasingly important (e.g., standardized surveys). Our treatment of some techniques has been rendered obsolete by advances in technology (e.g., still photography). And new aspects of the study of culture that were literally unheard of two decades ago (e.g., those dealing with communities that exist only in cyberspace or whose complexities can be studied only with up-to-the-minute computer applications) have now moved to center stage. A simple revision of the *Handbook*, then, would clearly not do. Julia Crane and I decided that instead of trying to write a new version of the book, I would edit a collection of essays by an invited panel of colleagues and friends—successful and innovative ethnographic researchers all—each addressing an ethnographic data-collection technique in which they had specialized. In this way, the expertise of various people actually doing current research would be brought to bear on the topic of field research.

Despite this change in organization, the underlying philosophy of the book remains unchanged. Each chapter is built around an exercise/project that readers can undertake to better see for themselves how basic textbook and lecture information is collected and analyzed by ethnographic researchers.

THE PLAN OF THE BOOK

Each chapter in the book begins with the author telling about a particular research project with which he or she has been involved. Although that project almost always involved multiple data-collection techniques, the author demonstrates why particular research questions were effectively answered employing one particular technique. He or she then goes on to present a brief history of that technique—how it developed, in what kinds of research contexts it has been applied. Next, he or she walks readers through a step-by-step discussion of how the technique is typically carried out. A very important part of this discussion entails the ethical implications of research. The primary ethical responsibility of any ethnographic researcher is to respect the dignity and privacy of those being studied; each data-collection technique presents its own particular challenges to the fulfillment of that ethical imperative. In each chapter, students are reminded to seek their instructors' guidance with regard to any specific ethics requirements that might apply in their own setting (e.g., rules about informed consent that might be monitored by a university's institutional review board). Each chapter ends with a suggested guided project for readers to follow.

The chapters are not written as scholarly treatises, and there are no footnotes (although each chapter includes a very brief and highly selective list of recommended follow-up readings). The aim is to give readers just enough information to appreciate the technique and its potential for use by social scientists, and then to go on to practice it for themselves. The exercise projects are written so that even students in beginning survey courses can work them, although instructors in more advanced courses can certainly suggest ways in which they can be modified to suit the needs of students with more background. Although almost all of the contributors are anthropologists, the projects are written in such a way that they can be applied by students of any other discipline that uses the ethnographic method. Most of the projects are designed to be completed by a single student, although a few seem to work best as team efforts. It is highly unlikely that any one student could possibly complete all the exercises in a single academic semester; the instructor will have to decide how many, and which ones, to assign in any given course.

One further disclaimer: there is a very wide assortment of data-collection techniques available to the contemporary fieldworker, and this book does not attempt to cover all of them. But a student who becomes comfortable with the fundamental methods that are dealt with herein will certainly have developed an effective repertoire that will remain the heart of any subsequent field research, and upon which other creative and innovative methods can be built.

The book begins with a chapter by Tierney on participant observation, perhaps the most traditional, most widely revered, and most widely misunderstood approach to conducting ethnographic research. Presentations of two other very traditional techniques (the genealogical method by deRoche and the life-history interview by Angrosino) follow. The chapter by Redfern-Vance takes note of the fact that these traditional techniques usually result in a massive amount of undigested narrative data (as opposed to easily sorted and analyzed quantitative data) and suggests some innovative ways to make sense of such material. A chapter on the use of archival records (including census data) by Rodriguez and Baber follows. This group of essays on traditional methods ends with Nanda's discussion of the uses of museum resources as an adjunct to ethnographic fieldwork.

The next six chapters deal with variously formalized, quantitative approaches that were not always necessarily part of the tool kit of traditional ethnographers, but that are very important to contemporary researchers (Persico and Borman, Puccia, McNulty, and Goddard on the study of formal organizations; Smith on free-listing vocabulary; Price on standardized observation; Baer and Weller on survey questionnaires; and Rees on demographic analysis).

Two essays follow that bring ethnography into the age of electronic communications. Bird and Barber describe doing ethnographic research on-line with communities formed by Internet chat groups. Wolfe and Hagen discuss the potential for using powerful, sophisticated computer modeling to analyze complex bureaucratic structures (although their suggested exercise allows readers the feel of such research on a scale amenable to simple calculations).

The last of the project chapters, by Berger and Ellis, is organized very differently from all the others. In recent years, the social sciences have been caught up in a thorough critique of their traditional methods, theories, and assumptions—a critique that often goes by the generic name "postmodernism." The basic proposition of postmodernism is that the objective reality so assiduously sought by social scientists is something of an illusion—the perceptions of even the most highly trained scientific analysts are inevitably shaped by their own situations (their gender, social class, racial or ethnic background, sexual orientation, and so forth) to the extent that all generalizations about social processes are essentially constructions that tell us more about the people who construct them than they do about the external reality they purportedly describe. Because that now-questionable objective external reality has for so long been encoded in standard expository scientific prose, postmodernists advocate the use of alternative means of presenting ethnographic reality— e.g., using the devices of fictional literature to describe social and cultural settings—and a more explicit insertion of their own identities into the analysis of those matters. The chapter by Berger and Ellis itself is written as a kind of "alternative" writing exercise; it is presented as a story, with dialogue and vividly described characters. The key elements of the other chapters (explication of authors' research projects, definitions of the methods used, guided exercises, suggestions for further reading) are included, but they are all woven into the larger narrative, rather than set out as explicit chapter sub-headings. As a result, the student will not only receive instruction on how to construct an "alternative" narrative account of cultural process, but will also have a model of the process in the way the chapter itself is written and presented.

The book's final chapter is not a project, but an invitation—an encouragement to participate in an ethnographic field school, particularly one that takes students into another culture for an extended period of time (usually a summer session) under the supervision of a faculty mentor. In this chapter,

Wallace discusses the benefits of participating in a field school and provides some helpful and practical advice on how to find a suitable school and get the most out of the experience. It is our hope that by completing some of the exercises in the rest of the book, students will come away with an appetite for more. The organized field school might well be an effective way to get that additional exposure to the sometimes frustrating, but always enlightening and personally enriching, enterprise of ethnographic fieldwork.

1

Becoming a Participant Observer

Gerry Tierney

A RESEARCH PROJECT

When I was a graduate student, the time came when I had to think about my dissertation research project. I knew that I wanted to design a project that would give me some insight into the daily lives of homeless people and I realized that the only way I could delve into those lives would be to live in the field. I had done some preliminary research in a homeless shelter in New York City, but ultimately decided to conduct my research in Anchorage, Alaska, a city where I had lived for twenty years and which I considered my home. When I was an undergraduate at the University of Alaska–Anchorage, I became interested in the indigenous people living in the metropolitan area. One of my professors, Linda Ellana, took me on a tour of the infamous Fourth Avenue area, the Skid Row of Anchorage, a street packed with seedy bars. Dr. Ellana was an expert on the Alaska Eskimos; she had lived in native villages and understood the value of experiencing the lives of people in their own setting. But she stressed the importance of understanding what is going on in your own backyard before thinking about going off to exotic places, as traditional anthropologists were supposed to do. She made me realize how fortunate we were to have indigenous people right in our backyard.

That night on Skid Row gave me many insights into a world that was previously hidden from my view, a world that was surprisingly viable, populated by people who were managing to survive despite great odds. That experience convinced me that whatever research I ultimately undertook, it would have to include participant observation in the daily lives of the people I wanted to study. And so I returned to Anchorage for my dissertation research.

PARTICIPANT OBSERVATION AS A TOOL OF ETHNOGRAPHIC RESEARCH

When I began my Fourth Avenue research I felt confident in my training in the skills of social research. On the other hand, I was frightened about entering this world. I would not be passing through, as was the case in New York, nor would I be there only for a brief tour under the supervision of a knowledgeable professor. I would be there essentially on my own for an extended period of time.

At first, my primary activity was just hanging out. I was usually quite comfortable doing so and I watched every little thing, always listening to the sounds of the street, a world that was slowly opening up to me. Through these means, I built some trust among the people and gained their cooperation in helping me learn about them and their activities. The only time I felt uncomfortable was when the tables were turned and people on the street took to watching me and asking me a variety of personal questions. During the first few weeks it became clear to me that I was the oddity on the street and that I was being observed and scrutinized with as much intensity as I myself employed while watching them.

Engaging people in conversation took a little more time, but it too eventually became an everyday activity. In this manner, I was able to begin hearing about my informants' views. I was also able to develop relationships with people that enabled me to interview them about aspects of their lives. One woman, an Eskimo, became a particularly good informant. She shared her life history with me, although she occasionally reminded me that there were some details of her life that she did not want published. ("This is for your ears only," she would tell me from time to time.) She was a woman with a rare and engaging sense of humor. She would frequently annoy me when she would announce in a voice loud enough for everyone in the shelter to hear, "Watch it! She writes." She did so with a twinkle in her eye and a hearty, infectious laugh. We developed a relationship based on mutual respect and trust. Being a participant in as well as an observer of the lives of people means that one has a responsibility to protect the integrity of those with whom one interacts.

My goal was to describe the everyday activities of a group of homeless people, with a focus on women. I wanted to know everything I could about the individuals who inhabited Anchorage's Skid Row. I wanted to know what it felt like to live in public places, how people could survive in such a seemingly hostile environment, and how they managed to get some enjoyment out of life all the same. These goals required not only an understanding of research methodology, but also a particular mind-set, a desire to see the world from the insiders' perspective. It is no accident that participant observation is the strategy used most often by ethnographic researchers to uncover the world views of people from cultures other than their own. While participant observation is certainly not necessary for all kinds of social research projects, it is an important technique for anyone hoping to develop relationships with, and not merely gather information from, those under study. In addition to hoping to write a scholarly dissertation, I wanted to be in a position to make some recommendations for the improvement of services to the homeless. I knew that my suggestions would have greater weight if I had lived through the relevant experiences so that I had a deeper understanding of and appreciation for the needs that the people themselves expressed.

I knew that I could not hope to see the everyday world of Skid Row women from their own perspective unless I shared that world with them over the course of time. To be sure, I was not able to participate completely, as some of the activities engaged in by street people are illegal and dangerous, especially for a woman. Nevertheless, the participant observation that I could do opened up the world of the homeless for me. In many ways, it is a world very much like my own, a world in which people have to be innovative, skillful, and clever if they want to survive. But the specific challenges to their capacities were ones that I had to learn about from the inside.

PARTICIPANT OBSERVATION: A BRIEF HISTORY

Prior to the nineteenth century, people interested in learning about foreign cultures had to read the second-hand accounts of missionaries, merchants, or other travelers. Many of these observations were ethnocentric, biased in favor of the culture from which the travelers came and tending to characterize foreigners as primitive or backward.

One of the first important observers of a non-Western culture to attempt to participate in that culture and understand it on its own terms was Henry Schoolcraft, a government agent working among the Chippewa Indians of the upper Great Lakes region in the 1820s and 1830s. Most Indian agents of that era had little interest in or respect for the native cultures, but Schoolcraft was cut from a different cloth. He learned the Chippewa language and lived in the villages and ultimately shared his intimate, encyclopedic knowledge of the culture in a series of books that detailed the history, traditions, customs, language, and social institutions of the people. He became a friend of many people in the villages, and on occasion found himself in the position of a political advocate who argued on behalf of Indian causes.

Although Schoolcraft was not a trained anthropologist, his work among the Chippewa illustrates the major aspects of what was to become formally recognized as the participant observation approach to ethnographic research. Participant observation is not simply a matter of living in close proximity to the people one wishes to study; after all, traders and missionaries often lived among the Indians, but made little or no effort to understand their culture in all its complexity. Participant observation is not just the collection of data, but a way of thinking about the people from whom one collects those data. It is also a way in which one perceives one's own position in relation to the people and the culture one is studying. Cultural relativism is a philosophical position that goes hand in hand with participant observation; its major premise is that no culture is superior to any other, and that each culture must be understood and evaluated in its own terms. Later in the nineteenth century, anthropologists in both Britain (e.g., Bronislaw Malinowski) and the United States (e.g., Franz Boas and his students, among whom perhaps the most famous was Margaret Mead) formalized the participant observation strategy and the principle of cultural relativism and made them the centerpieces of scientific ethnographic research.

PARTICIPANT OBSERVATION: THE PROCESS

The Skills of a Participant Observer

When I first read that some of the major skills involved in participant observation were watching and listening, I knew that this mainstay of anthropology was well suited not only for my project, but also for my personality. I am a patient person in most respects and I enjoy interacting with a variety of people. Before I entered the field, however, I really did not appreciate the importance of interacting with and getting along with people who, it turned out, would be active participants in my project. My training had always emphasized the activities of the researcher; I had to learn through experience that people from other cultures are not pliable puppets performing for me as a researcher; they are living human beings who quite often demand something in return from the researcher.

One of the biggest shocks for me in the field was the realization that I would have to spend a prolonged period of time living among people so seemingly different from me. I was not really prepared to deal with my own foibles and negative characteristics, but I had to do so—unless I understood myself better, I could not hope to bridge the perceived gap between myself and the people I was learning about. Fieldwork based on participant observation is a two-way street: just as I had expectations of the people (that they would share their experiences with me and honestly answer my questions), so they had expectations of me (to be honest and forthcoming about myself and my motives).

When you live for an extended period of time with people who seem to be very different from yourself, it is a good idea to watch out for feelings of superiority. While feelings of unease, suspicion, even a bit of hostility are only natural, they must be dealt with forthrightly and consciously set aside, lest they color the research in unwanted, negative ways. Indeed, the process of building rapport took up the bulk of my time early in the project, as I had to learn not only what the people I was studying were like, but also what *I* was like. People did not always want to be bothered by my silly questions and I had to learn that my own agenda, as important as it was for me, was not the only agenda that had to be acknowledged and dealt with.

As I reflect on my field experiences, I realize that another important aspect of fieldwork for me was that I was somewhat naïve. Some anthropologists go so far as to advocate cultivating naïveté. I am not sure one can consciously do so; perhaps it is sufficient simply to use the naïveté with which most of us come equipped and not try to overcome it or overcompensate for it. A certain degree of humility is required to do so. It is not, after all, easy to be in the position of one who appears to be constantly in the dark about even the simplest situations. Putting yourself in the position of the student, letting insiders teach you about the intricacies of their culture, is sometimes difficult, but in the end it pays off. You may, of course, have more "book learning" than they (i.e., you will almost certainly have read the available literature on the culture before beginning your fieldwork), but you cannot hope to see the world as they do if you constantly impose an "I know better because I read the book" attitude on every encounter. In my own case, the street people had long since learned that university types tended to be haughty, arrogant, rude, useless, and not very bright about survival on the streets. They frequently told me that nothing good ever came from one of the seemingly countless studies conducted on the streets of Anchorage. My willingness to be humble made me a much more acceptable presence.

It is also important to cultivate a sense of humor, which can help you put yourself and your work in an appropriate perspective. Extended fieldwork can be tedious at times, exhausting at others. Appreciating the ludicrous or incongruous aspects of the work can be a great blessing. When I was on the street in Anchorage, I learned how important a sense of humor was for the native people who became my friends. I was raised in a somber, puritanical, Irish Catholic household in Massachusetts. My sense of humor was never allowed to blossom; indeed, any kind of levity was looked upon with a great deal of suspicion. Early in my research, however, an Eskimo man pointed out that I never laughed out loud. He observed that I would smile and say, "That's funny," which he thought was very peculiar behavior. When I saw myself through their eyes I realized how strange I must have seemed and I made real efforts to lighten up and share a good laugh with my friends.

One additional skill is necessary for a good participant observer: writing. It is most important for you to write down, sometimes in excruciating detail, all your observations. Doing so has become much easier since the advent of computers, but it still takes time, discipline, and organization to sit down and write at length, every day. So if you do not like to write, or think you are not a very good writer, be sure to take time to practice before you enter the field.

The Stages of Participant Observation

The first step is to decide on a topic. Doing so may sound simple, but because it is a great, big world, and anything human in it is fair game for an ethnographer, it can be difficult to narrow your focus down to something that is doable. One good way to begin is to read about projects carried out by other researchers; you may wish to duplicate one of them in your own area, or you may wish to follow up on some suggestion an author has made. It is important to read as much as possible so that you can identify gaps in the literature, trying to fill in some area of knowledge not already well established. For example, when I began immersing myself in the literature on homelessness, I was struck by the fact that almost all of it dealt with men; there were surely homeless women, but we knew very little about them at that time. Choosing a topic and choosing a site for research are linked processes. In my own case, my prior interest in Alaska natives confirmed my decision to study homeless women in Anchorage rather than in New York.

Selecting a site is not, however, the same thing as gaining entrance. One does not simply show up somewhere and commence participant observation. It is usually desirable to have some trusted person or institution in the community you want to study help introduce you to the people. In my case, I decided to contact a homeless shelter and inquire about the possibility of serving in some capacity as a volunteer while I conducted research. The director of the shelter responded favorably. Nevertheless, my first day in the field was still stressful and anxiety-provoking. It was a very cold January day, and since the shelter did not open until late afternoon, I thought I would just hang around on Fourth Avenue to observe. You might think that a person who had lived most of her life in Alaska would have known better! It is just too cold to be outdoors in January. So I found a fast-food restaurant located right across the street from Skid Row. I drank a lot of coffee and ate a lot of French fries that day. I also felt depressed and wondered what I could have been thinking of to put myself in this awkward position. I found myself gazing off to the beautiful, snow-capped Chugach Mountains, and wondering, "What am I doing here?" I had some doubts about my ability to carry out the project. Anthropologists refer to such emotions as "culture shock."

Things did not get much better once I finally got to the shelter. The director was not on the premises when I arrived, and no one else seemed to know who I was or what I was doing there. So I just sat there trying not to look conspicuous. I continued to be plagued by feelings of inadequacy. Finally, a woman who worked in the kitchen approached me and graciously invited me to join her for a cup of coffee while she prepared the evening meal. She saved me from the stares of all the people entering the shelter and she eventually became one of my best friends. She was a Roman Catholic nun who was the only paid female employee providing direct services at the shelter. She was also the only advocate for women at this particular shelter—a role that, alas, led to her abrupt dismissal just a few months later.

And so with a great deal of frustration, I began what would be a field experience of six months' duration. This first day was not typical of the days that followed, but the major problem became quite clear to me on that day: I would have to interact with these people at the shelter on a daily basis and participate in their daily activities. It was a frightening prospect because I was not at all sure I had what it would take to complete the project.

One of the most difficult aspects of the work was a lack of privacy: I was almost always surrounded by people. After people got over the novelty of seeing me hanging around all the time, they began to treat me like an insider. On one level this sounds like a good thing, but it was troubling in some ways, in that I was treated like many of the women on the street—that is, as a person targeted for sexual abuse. Being a street woman meant that you were subject to a daily diet of sexual jokes, advances, inappropriate touching, harassment, and other forms of abuse at the hands of a variety of males—not just homeless men, but also men who were supposed to protect and serve them, such as police officers and social workers. It was important to have a sense of myself and to set limits about what I could, or would, participate in.

Although scientific research is expected to be objective, participant observation of necessity introduces a degree of subjectivity into the process. When you spend a considerable amount of time in the field with people, you grow close to certain individuals. One woman in particular was very intelligent; without her assistance I would not have understood much of what went on in the shelter and on the streets. This woman, Mariah, was not just an "informant," but a friend. Over the years when I return to Anchorage, she always throws her arms around me to welcome me back. I would not have been able to have conducted my research without Mariah; she may not always have understood why I wanted to be part of their lives, but she was always most generous in sharing herself with me. Participant observation is always a joint effort and it requires mutual trust and respect.

In warmer weather I would be on the streets until about 1:00 A.M., at which time I returned to the shelter to write up my recollections of the day's activities. I carried a little notepad in my pocket at all times and I would frequently write down key words or phrases that I would use in the evening to remember as much as possible. It would usually take a few hours to write up even relatively brief daily notes, which would then be used to write more expanded commentaries after a week or so. At times I thought I was drowning in minutiae, but when I was finished with fieldwork and began to write my dissertation, I was very happy that I had tried to record every last detail.

That final write-up—whether it is a dissertation, or a more limited course assignment—entails more than writing; it is a process of thought and reflection as well. There is a lot of organizational work that needs to be done, as your notes are likely to be very extensive. You need to decide how to categorize the notes so that you can efficiently retrieve data on particular topics.

YOUR PROJECT

This project needs to begin early in the semester, as participant observation requires more than one or two visits to a site. It might take some time just to set up the project and obtain permission to work with the people you are interested in studying.

In choosing your topic, do not undertake fieldwork in a situation that makes you nervous or uncomfortable. This first project should be enjoyable. If you do not deal well with conflict or aggression, you may want to avoid fieldwork in a jail, police station, or even a homeless shelter. If you cannot stand the sight of blood, a hospital emergency room is not for you. If you are unsympathetic to organized religion, fieldwork in a church, synagogue, mosque, or temple might be unpleasant. On the other hand, those settings might be perfect for you, depending on your interests or emotional resources. Remember that even sites as apparently mundane as laundromats have made for very interesting ethnographies—use your imagination in selecting both a topic and a site. Some examples from my own students include observations in tattoo parlors, fire stations, and diners. Some of my students are older, working individuals who conduct research associated with their jobs or their children. For example, one student conducted fieldwork in her son's computer science lab at a local secondary school. She not only provided the school with a detailed study of computer lab use, but also included recommendations for increased usage.

Depending on the site you have selected, you may need to contact someone in the environment to see if you would be welcome to hang out there. Some settings selected by my students (e.g., a day-care center) required very formal permission; others are more flexible, although it is always helpful to have someone who is already a trusted insider in that community be the one to introduce you to the others. If you choose some sort of service agency (e.g., a soup kitchen), you should consider volunteering some of your time, so that you are giving something back to both the staff and the clients and not simply hanging out selfishly doing your own thing. By all means, consult with your instructor regarding your school's norms for informed consent in projects such as this one.

Be prepared for some culture shock the first time you enter the field. Even if the place is familiar to you, you will be seeing it and interacting within it in very different ways. Whatever feelings of discomfort you may experience, try to remain as courteous as possible. Keep in mind that the people you are living/working among are providing you with both time and information. They are sharing part of their life with you, and without them you would have no project. Strive, therefore, to treat them with all due respect. An important part of showing respect is being honest about why you are there and what you are attempting to accomplish. If some people choose not to cooperate, do not take it as a personal affront and simply work with those who are more willing to interact with you.

Be sure to keep good notes. Depending on your personal preferences (and your resources), you may do so on index cards, a pad or notebook, or a Palm Pilot. Do not, however, spend all your time in the field with your nose buried in your notes. While you are in the field, use the cards or pads or other devices simply to jot down brief, simple reminders. You can flesh out these comments when you have some time to yourself. Do not put off that task, however, as you will lose many important details if you wait too long to transform the quick field note into a more circumstantial description.

Your final report should include a map of the environment you have been studying, as well as a detailed narrative description of the site. Do not take too much for granted (even if you are studying a very commonplace site); write your description as if for an audience of readers who are not familiar with the setting at all. You can then go on to write an interpretive analysis of what is going on in the environment, based in part on your own readings (how does this material conform to what I have read about other similar settings? how does it differ? why?) and on what your informants tell you about their own insights into their experiences. For example, one of my students chose to observe a local mosque; what particularly struck her was the way in which gender roles were played out in worship services and this aspect of the culture formed the core of her analysis.

Your report may also include photographs or sketches (if you have obtained the people's permission to use them), transcriptions of interviews, or materials pertinent to the site under study (e.g., brochures produced by a civic organization). By all means feel free to include any insights you have gleaned about your own personality in conducting this research.

A FEW SELECTED READINGS FOR FURTHER INFORMATION

Angrosino, Michael V., and Kimberly Mays de Pérez. 2000. Rethinking Observation: From Method to Context. In *Handbook of Qualitative Research*, 2nd ed., ed. Norman K. Denzin and Yvonna S. Lincoln, 673–702. Thousand Oaks, CA: Sage.

Jorgensen, Danny L. 1989. *Participant Observation: A Methodology for Human Studies.* Newbury Park, CA: Sage.

2

Exploring Genealogy

Constance P. deRoche

A RESEARCH PROJECT

About thirty years ago, I was looking for a field site where I could do research for my doctoral dissertation. Since my undergraduate days, I had been interested in economic development and social change. One day, a friend came to visit. He spoke about his home community, Benton (a pseudonym), a former fishing village that now found itself about twenty-seven kilometers (about seventeen miles) from a major heavy-industrial park. I was interested. With about 1,500 residents, the village was small enough to allow a single, novice researcher to work effectively. It was also accessible, lying just off a highway that passes through Nova Scotia's Cape Breton Island. Language proficiency would be no stumbling block, since the residents were fluent in English, although they were Acadian (people of French origin who live in three eastern provinces of Canada). Moreover, my friend and his family would introduce me to the community and help me establish rapport. After spending the summer of 1971 exploring the site, I was confident that I had found the ideal place to work.

Activity at the industrial park had begun late in 1959, when construction began on a pulp-processing plant, which finally opened in 1962. By the

19

summer of 1971, three heavy-industrial plants were also in operation, and by 1973 two of the park's plants had been expanded. During that period, thousands of construction jobs were created. In the end, more than 1,200 non-seasonal steady jobs (most of which were available to local people) had been produced, as had employment for about 1,000 seasonal pulp-cutters. Villagers were expecting another phase of growth that would place them in the orbit of a prosperous industrial magnet.

I wanted to learn how the industrial boom was affecting Benton, but I quickly realized that I would first need to know about previous conditions. Village history proved to be more complicated than I thought. Benton *had* been a fishing village, but that was only for a few decades after its settlement in the mid-1800s. For nearly a century thereafter, villagers pieced together a living by combining migrant labor, small-scale commercial forestry, occasionally available local employment, and subsistence production. As things turned out, I devoted a great deal of time to reconstructing past patterns of both paid and unpaid work.

While industrial development had brought a certain measure of prosperity to the region, it was clear that villagers had previously struggled to make ends meet. In fact, the industrial park was, in part, the product of government policies that aimed to stimulate economic development in poor regions. Those policies were the Canadian version of the "War on Poverty" being declared at the same time by President Johnson in the United States. In the 1960s, social scientists were engaged in lively debates about the causes of poverty. Anthropologists were becoming increasingly interested in examining poverty in their own society. In particular, a work by anthropologist Oscar Lewis provoked major controversy. Lewis had studied impoverished Mexicans and Puerto Ricans, as well as poor Latin immigrants in New York City, and he saw similarities among them. He concluded that in materialistic, achievement-oriented societies, economic deprivation led to the development of a "culture of poverty." The poor, he suggested, developed certain values and world views that kept them from prospering.

Anthropologists were also becoming more consciously aware of the relationships between the small communities they studied and the larger social worlds in which those relationships were embedded. Lewis's critics argued that the culture of poverty approach largely ignored the ways that poverty served the interests of advantaged people, as well as how poverty was produced by decisions made by powerful people to benefit their own interests. In trying to account for poverty, Lewis's approach, they felt, gave too much emphasis to poor people's states of mind and not enough attention to conditions over which the poor had little control. In short, it seemed as if Lewis was blaming the victims for their own plight. As a result of these criticisms, anthropologists declared war on the notion of the culture of poverty. Charles Valentine, an anthropologist at Washington University (in St. Louis) where I was studying, was among Lewis's most prominent critics. At Washington University, I had also worked as a research assistant to Alvin Wolfe, an anthropologist, and Lee Rainwater, a sociologist, both of whom were critical of the culture of poverty concept. Under the direction of Wolfe and Rainwater, I worked on a project funded by the Office of Economic Opportunity. Many of the people we interviewed for that study were rural migrants who came to St. Louis in the hope of improving their lot but found themselves living in material squalor. In addition, my own parents had been peasant immigrants from an impoverished region of southern Italy; they had worked hard and lived frugally in order to provide their children with higher education. In short, when I entered the field, I was already pretty skeptical of any explanation that seemed to blame the poor for their deprivation. What I discovered in Benton confirmed my skepticism.

I had also heard of the "brain drain" thesis—that is, the idea that the most talented and motivated people tend to leave impoverished regions for places that offer greater opportunity. This perspective also suggests that poverty is mainly the result of characteristics of the poor themselves. My graduate studies left me feeling that this thesis was simplistic. As I learned about the importance of labor migration in Benton, I became interested in assessing the role of brain drain in that community. The genealogical charts (or family trees) that I was constructing proved to be helpful in this regard, although I had not begun working on them for that purpose.

GENEALOGY AS A TOOL OF ETHNOGRAPHIC RESEARCH

When I started my study, collecting genealogical data seemed to be the natural thing to do. Anthropologists had always studied small communities in which kinship was important. Kinship was a core element in anthropology curricula even in the 1960s. It did not take me long to realize that villagers were connected to one another through a thick web of kinship ties. Neighbors were often relatives, since extended kin tended to cluster on inherited land. Kin were in frequent contact and were expected to help each other out whenever called upon to do so. Some married couples still lived in two-generational extended households, in dwellings that they would inherit (if their siblings had already moved along to households of their own). It made sense to construct genealogies in order to document kinship relationships among residents in a systematic way. Soon after arriving at Benton, I had drawn a rough physical map of the village, cataloguing households and recording the names of villagers who lived in each. By cross-referencing genealogical data, I was able to map relationships spatially.

I had been informed that the great majority of Benton's residents were descended from a few families that had settled the village. Establishing links to village founders was not, however, especially important for charting current, active relationships. The village kinship system was essentially North American in form: bilateral (that is, recognizing descent from both mother's and father's sides of the family) and generationally shallow (that is, tending to be restricted to two or, at most, three generations of ancestors, rather than going back to a mythical, totemic ancestor from ancient times). Many people knew a bit about their family heritage, and everyone knew that "we're all a little related here." The circle of effectively recognized kin, however, went no further than those who shared grandparents. Nevertheless, genealogies were useful in reconstructing village history. They led me to identify and to catalogue, in an organized way, past residents about whose lives (and work experiences) I could inquire. That is, constructing genealogies gave focus to my work with sharp-witted elders (especially one woman who was born in the 1880s), who acted as "key informants" about past work practices and migrant destinations. I asked them for data about ancestors' birth and death dates (some of which I was able to check against census and parish records and which proved surprisingly accurate). I was then able to generate retrospective but systematic and concrete data about how people in different time periods made a living and where they did so. Genealogies helped me identify those natives who had left the village for good. They revealed that a substantial number of natives (and their descendants) had done so, allowing the village to remain small and personal, a social condition that was valued locally. This trend also reduced pressure on family land that was used for small-scale subsistence farming and periodic commercial forestry. In fact, those who relocated did an economic service to their kin and, in a sense, a social service to the whole village. By asking where expatriates had settled, I could confirm generalizations about where villagers had gone in search of employment in various periods.

As my work proceeded, I realized that recurrent short-term labor migration was characteristic of virtually all those who continued to make Benton their home. Most villagers had begun migrant careers in their mid-teens. Upon marrying, young women left the paid workforce for housekeeping (often under arduous conditions) and an array of sometimes physically demanding subsistence-farming activities. Men, however, continued to engage in seasonal migration until age forced them to retire, except, on occasion, when local construction jobs were available or when job-market conditions in the larger society were bad (as during the Great Depression of the 1930s). In fact, villagers seemed to have an uncanny ability to find work in distant places, partly because of "chain migration"—relatives or friends who were living elsewhere would pass along word about work opportunities or help villagers secure specific jobs. Some men maintained ties to employers who would call them to work on fishing vessels or construction projects and sometimes ask them to recruit other workers. On the other hand, groups of men would often go on "guess work" to places where they thought job prospects were bright. Destinations changed as economic growth sites shifted. They also learned tricks to increase their chances of being hired, such as carrying well-used tools to suggest that they had a wealth of experience. They spoke proudly about the conditions they endured at work camps and about the gusto with which they applied themselves to job tasks. Very few people whom I interviewed expressed anxiety about finding work, despite its uncertainty. In fact, those who were nervous about it were held in some disrepute. The villagers' apparent stamina, courage, creativity, and ability to cope with employment insecurity made a strong impression on me.

In short, these people were by no means fatalistic, distrustful, complacent, work-shy, or lacking in self-esteem. I began to wonder whether their pattern of circular migration (going away and returning home) was actually a sign of character strength. Perhaps circular migrants were relatively self-assured and prone to taking risks. It seemed that the brain-drain proponents had it all backward. I therefore became interested in knowing how villagers differed from expatriates. Since most of the latter returned to visit relatives from time to time, I was able to speak to a few. They seemed unremarkable. I could not systematically interview the expatriate population, which was spread across the country and even beyond its borders. But genealogical data again came to the rescue. By using them I was able to discover that every sibling set contained both expatriates and local residents. No family line seemed especially ambitious about permanently sending away its members to make good elsewhere. In gathering kinship data, I collected information about where villagers' expatriate kin lived, their spouses' community of origin, and the jobs ex-resident men (or unmarried women) held.

My research suggested that on the whole expatriate men had not distinguished themselves in occupational terms, although the very few with outstanding levels of educational achievement found no appropriate local work until the recent industrial period. Moreover, marriage patterns exerted a heavy influence on residence. Village exogamy (the pattern of taking a spouse from outside Benton) greatly decreased the likelihood of settling back at home. When a man married a woman who had grown up in the community in which he was working, the couple was most likely to settle in that place. Those whose spouses were from neighboring villages might set up their households there or in Benton. But village exogamy discouraged settlement in Benton, because living there required periodic male migration, thus leaving the bride alone in a household and community to which she had no established ties. Since there were no rules defining where or with whom a couple *should* reside, exogamous couples very rarely settled in the village. In short, the kinship data suggested that resettlement decisions were not merely a sign of a drive toward economic achievement.

THE GENEALOGICAL METHOD: A BRIEF HISTORY

Collecting genealogical data is as old as anthropology. Lewis Henry Morgan, a founding father of the discipline, sent questionnaires about kinship to missionaries and government agents who were working with Native Americans in the mid-nineteenth century. Much of the debate about kinship systems in that era was based on indirect fragments of knowledge and on wild evolutionary speculation. In 1910, however, W. H. R. Rivers wrote a pivotal essay, "The Genealogical Method of Anthropological Inquiry," that described and promoted the systematic collection of genealogical data. Rivers argued that the method could be used to elicit information about kinship terms (the pattern of names applied to relatives); rules of descent, marriage, and residence; migration; and religious practices. The essay served as a guide for generations of anthropologists (particularly in Britain) who undertook firsthand field studies. Some ethnographers used genealogies as a way of discovering rules that guide and pattern behavior. Others became more interested in how people, as active agents, use the rules to promote practical interests, seeing rules more as products of behavior than as rigid producers of behavior.

Despite different theoretical perspectives, kinship was a central interest in anthropology for many decades. In fact, when in 1949 George Peter Murdock published his major work outlining forms of kinship systems, he called the book *Social Structure*. That choice of title may appear odd to you, as it did to me when the book was assigned as a text in my graduate kinship course. (I had been a sociology student in my undergraduate days.) But it makes more sense if we acknowledge that historically anthropology was much more focused on relatively isolated, small-scale (non-state) societies than it is today. Kinship in those societies was an important factor in structuring all sorts of social relationships, and hence was essentially the equivalent of the entire social structure.

Today, the world is getting smaller and local communities are ever more integrated into larger political and economic institutions. Formal government has taken over many functions once served by kin groups, and corporations organize economic life. Kinship has largely become a private matter. People have also become more mobile, and they often leave home and family to take jobs for which they are hired as individuals. They may find themselves living in communities where they are surrounded by strangers and they are likely to establish meaningful relationships with neighbors or co-workers to whom they are not related. In short, kinship, especially in urban industrial settings, *seems* relatively unimportant. It certainly cannot tell us all we need to know about how societies are organized, or about how they work. It is not surprising, then, that the genealogical method of inquiry has lost its central place in anthropology's methodological tool kit. It is, for example, rarely or barely mentioned in introductory texts (whose coverage of research techniques is limited to begin with). In fact, when invited to propose a topic for this volume, I suggested three possibilities. The editor encouraged me to opt for genealogy because he did not expect any other contributor to offer to write on the subject. But he thought it deserved coverage. I hope that my reflections on the village of Benton have proved him right.

Keep in mind that kinship ties continue to serve as a significant resource in many urban neighborhoods (especially poor ones) in both industrialized and underdeveloped nations. Moreover, migration is, if anything, more common than ever. Today we speak about our postmodern world in which populations disperse and geographical boundaries dissolve. Studies that focus on kin-based communities are rare. Anthropologists have become interested in social networks (connections between people who have few if any relationships with one another) that readily cut across space. While these networks may not be restricted to kin, kin are certainly important components of them. Kin networks form an important channel through which resources flow. In short, while genealogical data cannot catalogue all, or perhaps even most, of the relationships that are important to people, kin connections cannot be ignored by social researchers. As long as we understand the limitations of the genealogical method, and depending on the social processes we want to explore, genealogies can still contribute to anthropological research. And it is worth noting that many people are now taking up genealogy as a hobby; reconstructing one's own family tree is a satisfying enterprise for lots of folks who are concerned about losing touch with their roots in an increasingly rootless society. So learning how to collect genealogical data and construct usable genealogies (kinship charts) in an efficient and coherent manner serves even those who are not primarily interested in anthropological research.

THE GENEALOGICAL INTERVIEW: THE PROCESS

Some genealogical data are available in documents, such as parish records. But even amateur genealogists will typically want more than can be found in archives. In anthropology, the family tree or genealogy or kinship chart is just a way of organizing and compactly illustrating information that goes well beyond identifying ancestors. To find out about active, ongoing relationships among ordinary folk, genealogical researchers need to conduct interviews. In its basic form, the genealogical interview is like any other interview discussed elsewhere in this book. But there are some important points relevant to this particular type of interview.

First, in choosing a topic, think about family relationships you might enjoy exploring. Perhaps you read about a practice that interests you, such as arranged marriage, and you know someone from a community that has followed that custom. You might want to know if the custom is changing. Have younger people in a family from that community begun to have greater say in the matter or to choose their own spouses? Your personal experience might also suggest a topic. Your own family may have started using e-mail or bought a long-distance telephone plan. Are these changing the way people communicate with relatives who live at a distance? You can ask someone to compare how news flowed within the family before and after he/she started using new technology. Or, your family might talk politics a lot at the dinner table, and you wonder whether people tend to vote for the same political party as their kin. You may have heard a news story claiming that people tend to give most support to charities that serve a need that is felt by someone who is closely related to them.

Once you have settled on a central topic or theme, you can select a person to interview. For example, you may have decided to see if social status impacts family interaction. Do relatives who have better paying, more prestigious jobs tend to mix more with one another than with kin who do less well economically? You would then want to choose someone with relatives who are in different social class positions. In short, choose a respondent who represents a population or who is in the circumstance about which you want to learn. Working with someone you already know is convenient, but it can be awkward to switch from a personal relationship to a professional one for purposes of the interview. There is also a tendency for the person you are interviewing to assume that you already know certain information, which can then be omitted. So it might be better to work with someone about whom you have fewer preconceptions. In general, choose someone for whom the interview will not be a burden, who has the time and capacity to speak to you, and who is interested in doing so.

Having selected a potential interview subject, contact that person to explain your project in brief and to request participation. Describe the general theme of your study rather than the results you expect (e.g., "I want to learn about family ties among immigrants," rather than "I want to show that people retain strong family ties even when they live far apart"). If you presuppose your findings, you may inadvertently encourage people to tell you what they think you want to hear. You may also risk making them defensive, if their experience is not what you anticipate. People can be sensitive to the implication that they have not lived up to their family obligations or have given preference to kin that society does not condone (i.e., nepotism).

Most people enjoy talking about themselves and their kin, but your respondent may want to know how much time you will need. You can explain that the time commitment will depend on how much the person has to say, but warn her/him that you will likely need a few hours, and may even ask to make a return visit.

Do some background reading pertinent to the topic of your choice. For example, if you want to examine how people interact with kin who belong to a different social class than themselves, read a bit about social stratification. Think about how you would categorize the class position of your respondent and her/ his kin. Use your reading as a guide only—do not prejudge your results.

Write a preliminary list of questions about the factors you want to explore. The questions should be fairly specific and should avoid technical terminology. For example, if you plan to study economic reciprocity, you should not suppose that the respondent knows the term or, if he does, that he shares your definition of it. Rather than ask, "Does your family engage in reciprocal exchanges?" you would be wise to ask about whether and how your respondent's kin "help each other out from time to time," or how they "share things." If they do, you can ask about the sorts of things that they do and give, and get estimates about how often they do so. But do not become too wedded to your questions. Prepare yourself for surprises, since people's actions rarely fall neatly into categories that suit the researcher. For example, if you plan to use the genealogy to study migration, you will want to know where your respondent's relatives reside, and when they left home. But you may ask, "When did your oldest brother leave home?" only to find that he has come and gone several times. Genealogical interviews are relatively structured, since they catalogue a specific set of relationships. But take advantage of anthropology's more open, flexible approach to interviewing, which encourages researchers to add queries, modify them, throw out unproductive ones, and take up unanticipated themes that are meaningful to the respondent.

Review the alphabetic abbreviations that anthropologists use to denote primary kinship relationships. This shorthand will help you when taking notes during the interview, as well as when you actually draw the kinship chart. Standard abbreviations include the following: M=mother; F=father; D=daughter; S=son; Z=sister; B=brother; H=husband; W=wife. These symbols can be combined to allow precise designations of other kin. For example, you can distinguish different relationships that fall under the same term of reference, such as your "aunt," who could be either your MZ or FZ or MBW.

When you meet your respondent, take a few minutes for casual chat that will put both of you at ease. Briefly review the goal of your research. Be sure you have checked with your instructor about your school's policies about acquiring the informed consent of respondents and follow the guidelines carefully. Be sure to ask the respondent for permission to tape the interview, since being recorded inhibits or embarrasses some people. Remember, too, that you should not let yourself become passive, trusting the tape to capture all needed information. If you become inattentive, you will dampen the respondent's enthusiasm. You will also miss gaps in the data, ambiguities in answers, and opportunities to ask follow-up questions. So even if you are taping the interview, it is a good idea to take brief notes as a back-up. You might explain that you will construct a family tree as a way of organizing the information that the respondent is generously providing. You can show your gratitude by offering to give your respondent a copy of the tree when it is completed, since many people enjoy having them.

There is no strict sequence to follow in generating the data, as long as you remain systematic and thorough. Depending on the respondent's schedule and the size of her/his kin network, you may want to spend one session simply identifying kin relationships, and return at another time to ask about patterns of interaction or exchange. It is, however, more efficient and less confusing to ask your whole array of questions about each relative in turn. Use the alphabetic symbols noted above to describe the linkages that connect each relative to the respondent (e.g., FBD), and also record the particular cultural kin term the person uses to refer to a relative of that sort (e.g., "my first cousin"). The latter is especially important if you are interviewing someone from a non-Western or non-English-speaking culture. You can also get personal (first) names and use them in the interview to ease communication.

There is a difference between actual ties of descent and marriage and those which are culturally recognized and socially significant. Your job is not to document every knowable relative, but rather to discover how your respondent recognizes kinship and acts toward kin. If, as is most likely, you interview an English-speaking North American, you will quickly realize that there are no clear and distinct boundaries between kin and non-kin. "Close kin" fade into "distant" ones who, in turn, fade off into non-kin. Let the research discover where your respondent draws the line between kin and non-kin, or between different degrees of kin. Your respondent may indicate these distinctions explicitly as you catalogue her/his kin. The patterns of behavior that are described will also tell you about the distinctions being made. For example, your respondent may claim to have no special relationship with any of her cousins. But as you ask about patterns of interaction, you may discover that during special holiday seasons she always hosts her first cousins, but not her more distant ones. Your job is to figure out how your respondent thinks and acts with respect to kin. Do not, however, worry about gaps in your respondent's knowledge; no one in the world can reproduce a "perfect" kinship chart with every conceivable relative neatly in place.

Eliciting genealogical data can sometimes lead you into sensitive moral ground. For example, a respondent may be embarrassed about having been "born out of wedlock." Or you may suspect that a woman's "brother" or "sister" may actually be her own "illegitimate" offspring. A couple may be joined in a "common-law" partnership rather than a formal marriage. Many such irregularities were once considered scandalous, so even if you think nothing of them, do not assume that your respondent—particularly an elderly one— shares your tolerant view. Interviewers must be sensitive to signs of discomfort from respondents and respect their privacy. If your respondent seems uncomfortable, offer to move on or turn off the tape during the discussion of the sensitive material. Remember that your job is to gather *social facts* and not some sort of absolute truth. You are a social scientist, not a prosecuting attorney. If something comes up to which you do feel a moral objection, remember that you are entitled to your opinion, although you should restrain yourself from arguing with the respondent about it. It is all right to express your viewpoint, but not to the extent that you appear to be condemning your respondent and her/his life choices.

After the interview, make sure that you have properly labeled your tapes and protected them from erasure. Index your tapes by writing up a table of contents. Label each segment that pertains to a specific relative, using the alphabetic symbols as well as the person's name (to avoid confusion when there is more than one relative of the same type). Indicate where the segment lies on the tape, using minutes and fractions thereof. For example: MB, Bill Rivers, 2.5–4.5. Check your notes against the tape, amplify them when necessary, and list any ambiguities or apparent errors about which you should consult your respondent.

Review the graphic symbols that anthropologists use to draw kinship charts. The basic design includes a triangle to indicate a male, a circle for a female, a square for a person whose gender is unknown or irrelevant to the research question, an equal sign to indicate the marriage bond, a horizontal line for the sibling bond, and a vertical line for the bond between parents and offspring. A slash mark through the equal sign indicates a divorce. A slash mark through one of the figures indicates that the person is deceased. A dashed line indicates the adoption of children or siblings. Your respondent is conventionally labeled "Ego," the person to whom everyone else on the chart is related, but you may want to consider eliminating it in the chart you give to that respondent, since the term "Ego" sometimes has negative connotations. You should refer to the manual by Schusky in the list below for more detailed instructions about drawing a kinship chart.

Draw the chart by hand unless you are very skilled in technical graphic design. Using graph paper can help you keep the generational lines straight. Depending on the size of the kin network, your chart might become quite wide. You may have to tape together sheets of graph paper to accommodate all the figures. Devise a system of graphics that serve as codes for any further information that is relevant to your topic. Symbols for individuals can, for example, be colored or filled in with line patterns to indicate some characteristic or condition (e.g., use green to indicate all those who left the village to find employment). If you need to convey more information than a simple set of graphics will allow, you can number each individual and then cross-reference them to a set of notes. For example, your project may be about how kin help each other out. You may have discovered that a relative like Ego's oldest brother helped her get a job and fixed her car twice in the last year; she in turn painted that brother's house. Suppose that this brother is relative number 8 on your chart. The corresponding note 8 can then contain a short description of these service exchanges:

8. → helped get job, 9/98; twice fixed car, 1999
   ← painted house, 1999

Feel free to be creative and design a system that works to convey information efficiently and clearly. Whatever system you use, however, be sure to provide a legend, a list of each symbol and its meaning. For example, in the above note I used → to mean "help provided to Ego."

YOUR PROJECT

Using your knowledge (e.g., from other courses), your personal experience, and your imagination, choose a topic that can be investigated through the genealogical method. Although you might ideally need a number of informants to help you answer your research question, remember that this project is an exercise designed to help you practice the data-collection technique. So you will need to select only one or two respondents. Write up a brief statement of the theme you want to explore and explain why you have chosen this topic. Use clear, simple, ordinary language, since the statement will serve as your guide when you explain your purpose to your respondent.

Do some background reading on the topic and, on that basis, write up a set of questions. Then identify and contact your respondent, explain your request for her/his participation, and find a mutually satisfactory time and place for the interview. Review the alphabetic abbreviations for primary kin, and after getting the respondent's informed consent (and permission to tape, if need be), conduct the interview session(s).

Make sure that your tapes and notes are properly organized, review the graphic notations for drawing a kinship chart, and then draw a chart based on the information given to you by your respondent. Devise a system of codes for indicating pertinent information (either graphically or by means of numbered notes) and add these items to your chart. Provide a legend for your code. If you have used only graphic markers on the chart itself, place the legend in a corner of your chart. If you have used numbered notes, place the legend at the top of your note page. Write up any notes that you will offer. If you have promised to give your respondent a copy of the family tree, deliver it in a timely fashion.

Your report to your instructor should include: a) your respondent's consent form; b) the statement of your topic and your explanation for your choice; c) your respondent's kinship chart with legend and notes as appropriate; d) a short essay in which you outline what you learned about your topic, as well as reflect on your research experience, discussing any problems you may have had with using the genealogical method and any observations you have made about its strengths and weaknesses.

A FEW SELECTED READINGS FOR FURTHER INFORMATION

deRoche, Constance P. 1985. *The Village, the Vertex: Adaptation to Regionalism and Development in a Complex Society.* Halifax, Nova Scotia: St. Mary's University Department of Anthropology (Occasional Papers in Anthropology no. 12).

Keesing, Roger. 1971. *Kin Groups and Social Structure.* New York: Holt, Rinehart and Winston.

Murdock, George Peter. 1949. *Social Structure.* New York: Macmillan.

Pasternak, Burton. 1976. *Introduction to Kinship and Social Organization.* Englewood Cliffs, NJ: Prentice-Hall.

Rivers, W. H. R. 1910. The Genealogical Method of Anthropological Inquiry. *Sociological Review* 3:1–12.

Schusky, Ernest. 1972. *Manual for Kinship Analysis*. New York: Holt, Rinehart and Winston.

Stacey, Judith. 1990. *Brave New Families: Stories of Domestic Upheaval in Late Twentieth Century America*. New York: Basic Books.

Stack, Carol. 1974. *All Our Kin: Strategies for Survival in a Black Community*. New York: Harper and Row.

Valentine, Charles A. 1969. *Culture and Poverty: Critique and Counterproposals*. Chicago: University of Chicago Press.

3

Conducting a
Life History Interview

Michael V. Angrosino

A RESEARCH PROJECT

In 1980 I received a postdoctoral fellowship from the National Institutes of Mental Health, which wanted to help social scientists learn more about how public policy in the United States is formulated, implemented, and evaluated. During the fellowship year, I was affiliated with the Institute for Public Policy Studies at Vanderbilt University. Because Vanderbilt was home to a major research unit devoted to mental retardation, I turned my attention to that aspect of the larger mental health realm. At the time of the fellowship, mental health policy had just taken a new and exciting turn away from treatment based in large institutions and toward care based in community agencies. The "deinstitutionalization movement," as it was called, reflected a philosophy drawn from the civil-rights and other liberation movements of the 1960s and 1970s—all people, including those with various conditions considered disabling, had a fundamental right to live their lives in the least restrictive possible environment and to gain access to all necessary public services with a minimum of obstacles. This philosophy was made possible in the lives of people with chronic mental illness and mental retardation by advances in pharmacology—new medications that alleviate behavioral symptoms so that it is possible to live without constant, institutional supervision. An economic factor also played a part in the deinstitutionalization movement: allowing people with disabilities to live in their own homes was thought to be considerably less costly than maintaining them full time (often for their entire lives) in large, high-maintenance institutions.

In order for deinstitutionalization to work, it was important for necessary services actually to be available in local communities. In addition to their medications, people with mental retardation needed housing, transportation, employment, and education. We all know how complex modern society is and we recognize how difficult it can be to make contact with providers of all the many services we may need to help us get through life. It is therefore not surprising that people who begin with mental deficits—and who have lived much of their lives in protective shelters where they never learned the skills needed to fend for themselves—were not entirely successful in making the transition from institution to community. A few years into the great deinstitutionalization experiment, there were numerous reports in the popular press linking the policy to an increase in the number of homeless, haphazardly medicated people with mental problems wandering the streets.

It was clear that there had been a lack of connection between the policymakers and the intended beneficiaries of the policy. As an anthropologist, I wondered what the clients themselves thought about what they needed and what would help them make a more successful transition. My question was treated with some skepticism by the policy experts: people with mental retardation, I was told, could not organize their thoughts or develop a coherent perspective on their problems—and even if they could do so, they were so limited in their ability to communicate that they could not meaningfully articulate their point of view.

At first, I lacked the firsthand experience that would have allowed me to challenge the received wisdom. Therefore, when at the end of the fellowship year I returned to my own department at the University of South Florida, I decided to work with a local agency that served deinstitutionalized people in order to get to know them and understand how they viewed their circumstances. Seeing things from the insiders' perspective is, of course, one of the hallmarks of the ethnographic method. So I came to be affiliated with an agency that I have called "Opportunity House" (OH) in various publications. It served a clientele composed of deinstitutionalized adults, all of them males in the age range 20–42 when I first began working with the program. They were all dually diagnosed: mentally ill as well as mentally retarded. All had been convicted of some felony since their deinstitutionalization and had been remanded by the courts to OH in lieu of a prison sentence. OH was established to help people who had thus far failed to achieve the goals of the deinstitutionalization movement, and its educational and psychotherapeutic programs were designed to give these men another chance to succeed in the community. The OH staff taught basic classroom skills (reading, writing, arithmetic), life skills (telling time, making change), and social skills. Job training was offered in a greenhouse, a landscaping service, and a thrift store operated by OH, which also helped its clients find apartments of their own when they had successfully completed the program.

I began my affiliation with OH as a classroom volunteer, assisting the teacher by working one-on-one with the students as they learned their basic skills. I also helped out at the store, provided occasional transportation services, assisted clients who were ready to leave the OH group home and move into independent housing, consulted with a community "buddy" program that paired up young adults with mental retardation with people of similar age at the university, and worked on various fund-raising projects. I was eventually asked to join the OH Board of Directors. I also conducted a number of research projects designed to evaluate client progress and to track former clients who had graduated from the program. These projects included both graduate and undergraduate students as research assistants. By working closely with the clients, I came to the conclusion that the stereotype I had instinctively rejected was indeed false. The OH clients certainly had a great many problems organizing their lives, and a number of them were not readily able to communicate their plight except in the highly formal context of therapy sessions. But many of them were quite cognizant of what was happening to them. They also had some pretty definite ideas about what was wrong and about how they wanted their lives to turn out.

THE LIFE HISTORY INTERVIEW AS A TOOL OF ETHNOGRAPHIC RESEARCH

In order to document these feelings more carefully, I turned to a traditional ethnographic data-collection technique: the life history interview. This technique will be described in greater detail below, but for the moment, let us consider a few basic points. First, when I work with those who share the stories of their lives, I get a sense of how they understand their own identities and place in the world. The process is not designed to be therapeutic in the clinical sense, although it can certainly have secondary therapeutic benefits. The opportunity to rethink one's life, discern patterns, and consider what it all means can be deeply satisfying (even if occasionally scary), even for someone who has some difficulty organizing his thoughts.

Moreover, conducting a life history interview allows me to see how people conceive of their relationships to the wider society, since, unlike a clinical interview, it is not focused on the details of one's "condition," but on all the circumstances that have affected one's life. We may have come up with our faulty deinstitutionalization policy in the first place because we concentrated on the disability as if it were a thing in isolation. But people experience their disabilities as part of a continuous flow of life and they interpret their situation against a backdrop of everything else they have ever experienced. A life history interview yields an extraordinarily rich body of information that allows us to view social problems as part of a normal flow of life and not as isolated events amenable to single, quick-fix solutions.

For example, as I recorded the life stories recounted by the OH men, I noticed that almost all of them were simultaneously preoccupied with and deeply confused about their status as adults. They all knew that chronologically speaking they were adults and yet they had never been allowed to act or express themselves as adults. Some of the men had been suppressed out of misplaced kindness (their caretakers believed that if they acted too independently they would do inadvertent harm to themselves); others were thwarted by people reacting out of ignorance or fear as a result of common stereotypes about people with retardation. In any case, the men understood that even a benevolent agency like OH was complicit in keeping them childlike unless it granted them the possibility of experiencing adult life on its own terms. The theoretical literature on mental retardation sometimes speaks of allowing clients the "dignity of risk"—the opportunity that everyone else has for making mistakes and learning from them. To deny any adult the possibility of learning from mistakes, even with the best of motives, is to deny him or her the possibility of truly being an adult.

The OH men were particularly concerned about sexuality as a component of adulthood. It is virtually impossible to live in our society without absorbing numerous, often contradictory, images and messages about sex. It is equally impossible to escape the conclusion that, whatever else may be said about it, sex is really, really important in politics, advertising, music, and so many other aspects of our culture. Even people with mental retardation take in these lessons. Although some people with mental retardation are physically incapable of sexual expression, the vast majority are biologically normal. But unlike other biologically normal young adults, they have never been allowed to explore their own sexuality. They have been the victims of two opposite, but equally stifling, stereotypes: it is widely believed that people with mental retardation are either helpless innocents who need to be protected from the difficulties of sexuality, or ravenous monsters whose sexual appetites, once unleashed, cannot be contained except by force. Both extremes undoubtedly exist—as they do in the general population. But most adults with retardation are—like many adolescents—simply confused about sex. The life histories I elicited from the OH clients were full of unrealistic expectations and inappropriate role models—not because the men were mentally disordered, but because they had never been given a chance to sort out their ideas about sexuality. No one had ever bothered to talk to them about it except as part of a checklist of "don'ts" in various institutional settings.

A focus on the disability of mental retardation per se is limiting, insofar as it is seen primarily in cognitive terms, the remedy for which is "skills"-based instruction. Important as such training undoubtedly is, it is not the whole story. By contrast, when we place the disability in the context of an entire life as the person retrospectively reconstructs it, we can see that more general concerns about being an adult often take precedence over the learning of specific skills. Using this insight, I was able to convince the OH staff to institute sexuality education as part of the curriculum. The program emphasized forming, sustaining, and making decisions about interpersonal relationships, rather than the mechanics of sex or details of anatomy.

THE LIFE HISTORY INTERVIEW: A BRIEF HISTORY

The life history interview was pioneered by cultural anthropologists—but readily taken up by sociologists, social psychologists, and oral historians—early in the twentieth century. In many cases it was used to provide data when no other ethnographic technique would suffice. For example, by the time anthropologists turned their attention to documenting the cultures of Native Americans, it was no longer possible to find many fully intact communities in which traditional practices and beliefs could be observed. Therefore, researchers turned to the surviving elders of decimated tribal societies. In telling about their own lives, the culture of which they were once members could be illustrated. In a similar manner, sociologists working in large urban settings would have been hard-pressed to meet or interview all the members of a community (of recently arrived immigrants, for example). So a few "typical" or "representative" individuals were chosen for intensive interviewing insofar as their life experiences could be illustrative of those of the entire group. In still other cases, individuals who were clearly *not* typical (e.g., chiefs, shamans, great artists) were interviewed because their achievements were said to represent the highest values and aspirations of the common folk in their communities.

Two general traditions eventually emerged when it came to conducting life history-based ethnography. One, usually (although certainly not exclusively) associated with North American scholars, featured the biography of the single individual, either a representative or an exemplary member of his or her culture. The other, usually the product of European scholars, featured collective portraits—portions of the life experiences of a number of linked individuals that were put together to form a kind of mosaic of the community as a whole.

In our own time, a certain philosophical skepticism has come over life history researchers. It is now no longer so easily taken for granted that the individual biography represents the culture in microcosm, or, conversely, that the group ethnography is the individual personality writ large. There is now a tendency to concentrate on the ways in which narratives are constructed, rather than on the specific content of the stories; indeed, it is often held that the content, far from representing documentable fact, is actually the product of complex influences (such as gender, race/ethnicity, or socioeconomic class) that can disguise more than it reveals. Nevertheless, it seems reasonable to conclude that most people who are asked to tell their stories do so without deliberate intention to deceive. We do, however, need to be cautious—material presented in a life history interview should never be taken at face value as the sole source of evidence, as the human memory is an imperfect thing. It should be cross-checked whenever possible by other kinds of archival or documentary evidence.

Despite these ambiguities, contemporary ethnographers have given new emphasis to the old life history method because it has proven to be an effective way to get the voices of previously silent people on to the historical record. Official history has, until recently, been a record of the activity and accomplishment of elites. Women, poor people, members of minority groups, and those considered "deviant" for any reason were all around and active while those elites were engaged in their business. But we rarely hear about them, except through secondhand reports. Since such people have not until our own time left much of a paper trail, the only way to recapture their experiences, and to add their viewpoint to the larger historical record, has been through *oral* history, of which the life history interview is an important component. As a result, ethnographers interested in the history and development of roles of women, racial and ethnic minorities, members of different socioeconomic strata, people with disabilities, or those of non-standard sexual orientation have made extensive use of life history interviewing.

THE LIFE HISTORY INTERVIEW: THE PROCESS

People are usually very eager to cooperate with someone who actually wants them to tell their life stories. As noted above, reflecting on one's life can be personally very satisfying, particularly when it can be shared with a sympathetic audience. It might therefore seem that there is nothing more to the life history data-collection technique than turning on a tape recorder and sitting back to relax while the storyteller spins the tale. But even leaving aside the particular problems inherent with working with people with mental deficits, the process is by no means so carefree. Being a good interviewer in any context requires being a good listener, which means being an active participant in the storytelling process, not simply an extension of the tape recorder. The following considerations all factor into the development of one's skills as a good listener.

First, you must choose a person to interview who has valuable information and who is able to convey that information in a reasonable manner. (Allowances can be made for people with mental retardation who have trouble expressing themselves, or older people who may suffer memory lapses. But such problems should not rule such people out of consideration if their life experiences can help illuminate some issue you are interested in learning more about.) The chosen narrator should be someone who doesn't mind talking and who is reliable (that is, someone who will show up for the interview and be prepared to address the topic at hand). Although it is sometimes necessary to approach a potential narrator through intermediaries (for example, if the person is in frail health or is a celebrity), it should always be that person with whom you make the final agreement to conduct an interview. Never depend on others to set things up for you all the way through.

Before the interview even begins, learn as much as you can about your narrator. The intention is not to trap the person in little inconsistencies, but simply to make you better able to put his or her comments into context, and to allow you to ask the most intelligent questions about his or her experiences. Phone or write the narrator in advance, spelling out your goals in a way that is clear to that person. (Remember that the academic jargon that we use in describing a research project is a foreign language to most people, even highly intelligent ones.) It is usually wise to avoid generalities. For example, don't say that you want to interview the person so as to produce his or her life history; most people do not consider themselves qualified to speak as historians, and in any case do not typically see their own lives as part of history— the very term can be intimidating. Say instead that you want to talk about "your experiences and the people you've known."

In addition to background research on your narrator him/herself, do some prior research on those topics that you expect will figure most prominently in his or her story. You need not become a great expert—indeed, it will be helpful if you can honestly seem to be in need of enlightening information from your narrator. But neither should you seem as if you are totally in the dark, since then the narrator will wonder why you are going to all the trouble of doing an interview on a topic that seems to mean nothing to you. Background research can help the interviewer ask informed questions, know what details to probe for, and be aware of both what is and is not generally known about the topic. It can help the interviewer avoid vagueness by uncovering new information. It also helps establish rapport by demonstrating some familiarity with material close to the narrator's heart. Sources of information for such background research might include: college libraries (particularly if they have special collections devoted to local history); government documents; county and church records; back files of newspapers; local historical societies; personal collections of old magazines, photos, architectural plans, and other mementos. The Internet is becoming an increasingly valuable source of information as well.

As you prepare for the interview, be sure to familiarize yourself with any equipment you may be using. Make sure that it is in good operating condition and that you know how to work it without making a big fuss during the interview. Most life history interviewers now work with inexpensive, small, battery-powered cassette tape recorders with built-in microphones. Using battery power rather than plugging into a wall outlet gives you greater mobility and flexibility. For example, if a wall outlet happens to be near a noisy air conditioner duct, your sound quality will suffer if you don't have the option of going somewhere else. (If your interview involves material that requires better sound quality—for example, if you are interviewing a musician and are recording his or her performance—you may need to invest in a better machine. Some projects also call for video, as well as sound recording. My remarks here, however, will be confined to basic tape recording.) See if you can get a machine with a "pause" button, which can turn the tape off and on during the interview without turning the machine off completely; repeatedly turning the machine off and on can damage the tape. Do not use "voice-activated" systems since they have a tendency to lag in pick-up and thus lose parts of sentences, particularly if the person is speaking in a relatively soft voice. Do use a machine with a digital counter and a battery-power indicator. Bring an ample supply of fresh batteries to the interview. Opinions vary on this point, but I recommend using 60-minute tapes. Tapes with longer playing times tend to be thin and subject to breakage. Choose a cassette in a plastic case that is bolted, not glued together. (If the tape gets tangled, it is easier to open a bolted case to straighten it out.) The case should be clear, not dark or opaque, so that you can more easily see how much tape is left.

Arrange a time and place for the interview that is mutually convenient and comfortable. Although priority should be given to the preferences of your narrator, keep in mind that you are an active participant in this interview and you should not feel inconvenienced or uncomfortable, lest your frustration spoil the atmosphere.

Before the interview begins, have the narrator sign a legal release form that spells out the aims and conditions of the interview, including expectations of what will happen with the taped record, transcripts (if any), and the results of the research (e.g., "a paper for my course that only my instructor will see," or "a book that will be published by a major international press"). Such "informed consent" is absolutely required when a research project involving human subjects is conducted under the auspices of an institution that receives federal funding, although classroom projects may be exempt. Even if the form is not mandated at your school, you should get into the habit of using one, to protect both you and your narrator. Your instructor will show you examples of release forms that are in use at your own school.

Tape a "lead" before starting the interview. It should consist of the date, name of both narrator and interviewer, location of interview, and a brief description of the expected content. The lead is useful when the tape is archived; it serves the secondary purpose of giving you something to play when you get to the interview to make sure that everything is operating properly.

Unless the person you are interviewing is very pressed for time, do not feel that you need to get to the point all at once. Allow yourself time to break the ice with ordinary conversation. Remember that good interviewing technique is essentially a matter of paying attention. Look at the person you are talking to. Meeting the narrator's gaze easily and frequently (but not constantly—no one feels comfortable when being stared at) and not allowing yourself to be distracted will indicate a sincere interest. Sit in a relaxed, yet alert position and try to control fidgeting or unnecessary fiddling with the tape recorder. It is important to be responsive, which can be indicated either verbally ("Yes," "I see," "Uh-huh" all indicate that you are paying attention), through gestures, or by facial expression.

It is a good idea to keep notes during the interview. You may want to jot down words or names whose meaning or spelling are not clear to you and that you want to check out later on. There may be dates or chronologies that you want to verify. You may also want to note details of the setting that might help place the narrator's words in some context. But do not become so immersed in taking notes that you fail to maintain your conversational tone. You are an interviewer, not a stenographer.

Try not to interrupt your narrator, even if he or she seems to be wandering off the topic. If you have chosen a topic of real interest to the narrator, then he or she will get back to it eventually, in his or her own way. And if your topic really is the person's whole life, don't be too quick to judge what is and is not relevant to the person's recollections. Some oral history guidebooks insist that the interviewer should never interject personal opinion. I do not agree. I believe that the interview is a kind of conversation, and while you certainly want to be careful not to hijack the narrative and turn it into *your* story, I believe that sharing some of your own experiences (whether they complement or contrast with those of the narrator) indicates your real interest in the topic and also gives the narrator some further food for thought, which could spark a response that might not otherwise have been forthcoming. And certainly if the narrator says something that is personally offensive, you need not feel obliged to let it go by without comment.

Don't be afraid of silences. A brief lag in the conversation is perfectly normal, and you should not feel compelled to fill every second with idle chatter. Sometimes people pause because they are trying to remember a specific detail, or because they have been overcome with emotion at the recollection of a particular person or event. The interviewer should respect such pauses and learn to distinguish them from an actual stop that indicates that the narrator does not care to continue.

Use open-ended questions whenever possible, because they call for descriptive answers rather than for brief bits of data. Try to practice framing your questions in a two-part format: in the first part, you explain why you are asking something, and in the second part you go ahead and ask it. (For example: "I've noticed that everyone in the group home has his own radio in his room. What kind of music do you like to play?") Doing so indicates that you are observant and putting the narrator's experience into context and not simply conducting a witness-stand grilling. Questions should not, however, be so open-ended that they become impossibly general. A question like, "What was your life like when you were at the hospital?" is simply too vague for most people to respond to meaningfully. But try not to get *too* specific—at least until you know the person better—lest you come off as overly nosy, prying into personal matters that the narrator feels are none of your business.

Ask only one question at a time. It is sometimes tempting, when you are truly interested and excited about a topic, to bombard the person with inquiries. But hold back: if you are afraid you will forget a question, jot it down for future reference—don't blurt out everything all at once. Avoid questions that seem to make an assumption about what the answer is going to be. For example, ask, "How were you treated in the foster home?" not, "How often were you beaten in the foster home?" There is a tendency for narrators to tell interviewers what they think they want to hear; in some cases, a narrator may deliberately do the opposite just to be ornery. By phrasing the question in as neutral as possible a manner, you are more likely to get an honest response. For the same reason, avoid questions that only require verification of information. (Ask, "How do you get to work?" not, "You get to work from the group home on the Number 4 bus that runs past the mall, don't you?") There is, of course, a tendency to be "helpful" when working with people with mental disabilities, or frail elders, and so forth, but even in such cases, don't be so "helpful" that you end up telling the story yourself.

Don't interpret your narrator's responses, particularly when it comes to emotional expression. For example, don't say, "You must have been very relieved when they sent you to OH and not to jail," but rather, "How did you feel when you were sent to OH?" Don't use emotionally charged words or turns of phrase (e.g., "How did you feel when the cops nabbed you?" seems to call for a negative response. It is better to ask, "How did you feel when you were arrested?"). Don't supply your own adjectives ("What did you think when you first saw this nice, clean group home?").

Above all, let your interview flow naturally. Avoid making it seem like a survey questionnaire. It is perfectly all right for you to have a checklist of questions that you want to deal with, but don't structure the interview so rigidly that your agenda becomes obvious. Sometimes the narrator's digressions will provide the most interesting and important material. Let your narrator's body language or actual verbal cues tell you when he or she has finished with a particular topic.

When the narrator indicates that he or she has nothing further to say, do not simply turn off the tape recorder and leave abruptly. Stay for a while to chat (if the narrator's circumstances—and your own schedule—permit). Sometimes the casual chat reminds the narrator of something he or she forgot, and the interview starts again. If your own schedule is such that you cannot stay longer at that point, make an appointment for a follow-up interview. Before leaving, take a photo of the person and the surroundings (if the narrator permits it and if doing so has been spelled out in the informed consent form). Check your notes regarding unfamiliar words or spellings that you need to verify.

Once you are back home, immediately label all tapes (both sides) with your name, the narrator's name, the date, time, and place of the interview. Number each side of each tape in consecutive order. File all signed release forms so that you can easily retrieve them. Remove the plastic tabs from the backs of the cassettes to prevent accidental erasure. After a day or two, write a letter (or e-mail, if appropriate) or make a phone call thanking the narrator for the meeting and confirming the follow-up interview, if there is to be one.

Although some people like to see full transcriptions of their interviews (and they may so stipulate on the informed consent form), it is rarely necessary to make and keep full transcripts unless you are publishing a complete autobiography. If your narrator does want to see a transcript, establish in the informed consent form whether or not he or she will have the option of editing the material before you use it in your report. Instead, most oral historians rely on indexing as a way to retrieve specific information from the tapes. Indexing by minute (using a stopwatch if possible) is best, since the meter/counter number may vary from one machine to another. Divide the tape into approximately five-minute segments, or by obvious breaks in the subject matter. Make the index as detailed as possible, and do it as soon as possible after the interview so that the material is still fresh in your mind.

YOUR PROJECT

In order to practice your skills as a life history interviewer, select *one* person whose life story you want to record. That person should be part of some larger group or community whose overall ethnography you are interested in studying. That group should be one that has historically been left out of the public record. My project with deinstitutionalized adults with mental retardation is only an example. You might be interested in learning more about the historical roles of women, or members of particular racial or ethnic minorities, or native people, or members of particular occupational groups. In any case you should select someone to whom you have easy access. Be careful, though, if you select a member of your family or a close friend—you are likely to take too many parts of the story for granted and will not be as attentive as you might be to filling in the gaps.

Write out a brief justification for your selection. This paragraph should indicate some larger topic and theme that you are interested in exploring. (For example, "I want to find out more about how refugees from Southeast Asia first came to our town because I studied the Vietnam War in an American history course. We learned a lot about the political and military perspective of the United States, but I want to understand how the war affected the people who actually lived there.") This initial interview is your way of entering that community or deepening your understanding of that issue. If you know the *category* of person you would like to interview, but don't know how to contact a specific individual in that category, consult with your instructor, who should be able to guide you to campus or other local links who can make an introduction for you. When you make your initial contact with the selected narrator, share your justification statement with him/her so that he/she understands why you think it is important to conduct this interview. For this reason, the justification statement should be written in plain language, not academic jargon.

Conduct the appropriate background research and develop a question guide. Set up and conduct the interview (in as many sessions as seem necessary) according to the principles suggested in the previous section. Take care of the housekeeping chores suggested for the period immediately following the interview and then proceed as soon as possible to the indexing of your tapes. Your final report to your instructor should include the index, accompanied by any photos or documentation that your narrator has given you permission to use. A copy of the signed informed consent form should be appended to your report. You should also write a brief essay in which you explain what you have learned about the narrator, about the group that he/she represents (or the historical event in which s/he participated), and about yourself as an interviewer.

A FEW SELECTED READINGS FOR FURTHER INFORMATION

Angrosino, Michael V. 1998. *Opportunity House: Ethnographic Stories of Mental Retardation*. Walnut Creek, CA: AltaMira.

Denzin, Norman K. 1989. *Interpretive Biography*. Newbury Park, CA: Sage.

Hoopes, James. 1979. *Oral History: An Introduction for Students*. Chapel Hill: University of North Carolina Press.

Ives, Edward D. 1974. *The Tape-Recorded Interview*. Knoxville: University of Tennessee Press.

Langness, L. L., and Gelya Frank. 1981. *Lives: An Anthropological Approach to Biography*. Novato, CA: Chandler and Sharp.

Thompson, Paul. 1992. *The Voice of the Past*. New York: Oxford University Press.

Yow, Valerie R. 1994. *Recording Oral History: A Practical Guide for Social Scientists*. Thousand Oaks, CA: Sage.

4

Analyzing Narrative Data

Nancy Redfern-Vance

A RESEARCH PROJECT

I worked in the field of women's health as a nurse-midwife before I became an anthropologist. Numerous women have shared intimate details of their personal stories and life experiences, both joyful and tragic, with me over the years. I listened to women as they described their feelings about their bodies, their place in the world, their critical life junctures, their transformative journeys, and their processes of aging. Women's accounts of violence and rape were especially difficult for me to process and absorb. When it came time to choose a dissertation topic, I applied for and was awarded a Veterans Administration (VA) predoctoral fellowship, funded through the VA Office of Academic Affairs, and elected to study sexual abuse of women veterans. Violence toward women had surfaced as a major problem in the field of women's health and was a key issue for the VA. Sexual abuse is costly to the military and VA in terms of decreased productivity, unused talent, health care treatment, and litigation. The predoctoral fellowship enabled me to complete this research project and provided me with office space, materials, and a stipend, as well as a whole network of research mentoring support at the James A. Haley VA Hospital in Tampa, Florida.

The percentage of women in the military has steadily risen, especially since the armed services became voluntary in 1973. The number of women entering the armed services and subsequently transitioning out as veterans continues to increase in proportion to men. More women veterans are served by Florida VA hospitals and clinics as a result. Florida was an ideal location for this study since it is second only to California in population of women veterans.

In 1992, the armed services introduced a "zero tolerance" policy with regard to sexual assault and harassment; nevertheless, highly publicized incidents like Tailhook and Aberdeen continue to surface. Research demonstrates the prevalence of sexual abuse of military women. For example, we have learned that a woman in the military has more chance of being sexually assaulted in her average four to six years of enlistment than a civilian woman does in her entire lifetime. The VA health care facilities are left to deal with the aftermath.

There are still a number of questions left to be addressed. For example, definitions of the term "sexual abuse" remain ambiguous and contested. Even contemporary feminist scholars cannot agree on a definition. To some, only overt forms of violent sexual abuse or clear abuses of power should be addressed as a political issue, with the rest kept on a personal level. Others extend the definition to include any sexual infraction, however minor it may appear, as a form of rape that should be fought publicly. Researchers and women's health advocates do agree, however, that the damage caused by sexual abuse can be costly, both personally and financially.

A missing link was a definition of sexual abuse that was meaningful to the women who have experienced it. I felt that examination of the problem from the standpoint of women veterans within a historical, cultural context would be critical to achieving positive changes in the approach to sexual abuse and other targeted issues facing women in the VA today. I set out to discover how military women themselves define sexual abuse as it occurs within the context of their lives and how their individual biographies intersected with the organizational culture of the military. In anthropology we explore issues as they occur in a particular historical, political-economic, and personal context. We are in an era in which "sexual harassment" is a household word and "sexual abuse" has leaped from closets onto family-room television screens.

My goal was to contribute to policy and programs for dealing with this complex problem. I experimented to see if narrative analysis was a method that could be used to make policy recommendations and design better programs for women who experienced sexual abuse in the military. I thought life histories were well suited for studying a topic as sensitive as sexual abuse. I was confident that with this personalized, unhurried, interactive, relatively informal style of data gathering, I could capture more illustrative data than I could with survey research. Indeed, the narratives elicited from nineteen women veterans taught me about the significant role culture plays in defining sexual abuse.

In order to identify participants, I sent letters of invitation that described my project to women veterans residing in the area. I was uneasy at first, knowing that the harm a woman suffers from sexual abuse is often compounded by the legal, economic, and medical systems of society. I did not want to add to any woman's distress, and so I arranged for VA mental health counselors to be available for the women if the interviews brought feelings to the surface they found difficult to handle. The women contacted me by phone or e-mail. Two who initially agreed to participate later changed their minds, saying that they feared the retelling of the incidents would be too difficult for them to deal with.

I conducted interviews with others at the VA who were professionally interested in this issue. I also attended VA research conferences and special programs for women veterans, and tagged along with military recruiters to observe their process. I toured the VA Benefits Office and veterans' outreach centers. All these activities helped me become more sensitized to the issue of sexual abuse in the military. I helped revise and analyze a women's violence screening questionnaire for the VA Women's Center. Doing so reinforced what I had read about the scope of the problem. Out of 686 new women veteran patients surveyed at the Women's Center between 1996 and 1999, 24.8% said someone had used force or the threat of force to have sex with them against their will. An additional 33.5% said they received uninvited and unwanted sexual attention, such as touching, cornering, pressure for sexual favors, and verbal remarks.

I usually began the interview by saying something like, "Everyone has a life story, and I'm interested in yours," or "Please tell me how you got from where you were when you were a little girl, to where you are now in your life, and include in your story your experiences in the military." The interviews were conducted in various settings. I asked the women where they would be most comfortable talking. Sometimes it was in their homes or offices, other times at my VA office or in a reserved library room. One interview took place in my home and another in an outdoor setting. The women selected their own pseudonyms. The interviews ranged from two to six hours in length. Every interview was audiotaped and transcribed verbatim. At times I felt I had entered a foreign culture, complete with its own language barrier. I found it helpful to construct a dictionary of military terms to define unfamiliar words or phrases I encountered in the interviews.

The veterans defined rape in terms consistent with the common legal definition, focusing on physical sexual assault; they saw it as clearly different from sexual harassment. Their definitions, however, became ambiguous when they tried to identify where tolerable flirting ends and harassment begins. A number of women were particularly bothered by what has been called "gender harassment" in the research literature. Such harassment may not be overtly sexual; it may entail the women being stereotyped and treated differently just because they are women. Defining a "hostile work environment" narrowly, by including only explicit sexual overtures, excludes some of the most debilitating harassment faced by the women. Their wounds were not limited to sexual assault and harassment. The veterans' definitions were broader and included harassment resulting from a double standard of treatment. There were also women veterans suffering from discrimination because they are gay or of a certain ethnicity. They encountered abuse that, while not necessarily sexual, still results from all these types of abuse and discrimination that they felt was damaging to them as women.

NARRATIVE ANALYSIS AS A TOOL OF ETHNOGRAPHIC RESEARCH

I confirmed to my own satisfaction that narrative methods could indeed be useful with policy research. Narrative research frees us from oversimplification and stereotypical assumptions when designing programs and policies. It has the potential to attract wider audiences and political attention because narratives grasp the human dimension and are more readable, interesting, and compelling than charts and statistical tables.

Applied anthropology is about finding answers that translate into problem solving. Where better to start than with those who are at the point of the struggle? People closest to the problem are often the first to think of workable solutions. We can develop better intervention programs and policies by understanding the individual meanings humans attach to particular life events. I was able to offer a number of program and policy suggestions for the VA health care system, the VA benefits division, and the Department of Defense human-resources planning offices.

An earlier chapter in this book has already described the process of collecting narrative data (in the form of life histories) and has explained the rationale for using such data in ethnographic research. This chapter focuses on the ways we can deal with those data. Narrative research (particularly a project like mine at the VA that involved interviews with as many as nineteen participants) yields a mass of information; in this case, the verbatim transcripts alone amounted to several hundred pages. Data from survey research come from even larger population samples, but they are relatively easy to handle because they are numerical in nature and fall into predetermined categories. Narrative data, by contrast, often flow in a stream of consciousness, cover many different topics and themes (especially if they are *life* stories and not simply focused interviews on highly selected topics), and do not necessarily fall into easily perceived patterns for analysis. I therefore want to explore the ways in which we can make sense of this extremely rich, but potentially confusing, source of cultural information.

ANALYZING NARRATIVE DATA: THE PROCESS

After completing my interviews, I found myself surrounded by stacks of pages of transcribed life histories, memos, and field notes. There is no standard method for analyzing such material, so I tried a variety of approaches that have been suggested in the research literature. Some scholars have compared narrative research to a choreographed production. I agree, and so gravitated toward those analytic approaches that allowed me to treat the narrative like an interpretive dance with a distinct form, signature moves, a connection with the audience, and an underlying rhythm.

After some particularly exhausting interviews, I recorded some notes in my car on the way home but could not face typing up those notes until my sadness over the tragic events narrated had subsided a bit. It became standard procedure for me to carry a small tape recorder at all times so that I could keep a running diary of thoughts and insights that occurred to me even before I had gotten around to a formal analysis of the material. I found it helpful to share some of these memos to myself with my dissertation advisor, just to get an objective outsider's reaction to something I had been told and to my reaction to that comment.

My main concern in analysis was not to fracture the narratives, but to preserve and study them within the holistic context in which they were told. I examined them as they were organized and performed by the narrators themselves. The women veterans tied together components of their life stories in their own individual fashions. They selected the way the narrative would unfold to get at the points they wanted to emphasize (e.g., some liked to get right to the point and begin with critical incidents; others preferred a more circuitous route, circling around important milestones and surrounding them with preparatory detail). They selected themes and the ways in which those themes were connected (e.g., some followed linear chronology, linking life events in a this-happened-and-then-as-a-result-that-happened format, while others leaped around, allowing something that had happened recently to trigger a memory of something in childhood that seemed in their minds to be related). They set the stage, selected the props, introduced the major characters, and narrated the script from their personal repertoire of cultural resources.

I looked first at classic structural approaches used in literary theory and was amazed to discover the diverse ways the women arranged their narratives into coherent forms. I was curious about what the women placed in the forefront and what they relegated to the background, so I created interpretive diagrams to help me visualize the diverse ways story plots were organized into global coherence. The organization of the women's narratives seemed to fall into one of five basic formats: spiral, time line, geographical map, series of dramatic scenes (not obviously related to one another), and chapters in a novel (dramatic scenes all of which revolve around a common theme or point). An example of the latter is Flora's narrative; her style is to introduce an overall theme, often in the form of a question she seeks to resolve for herself, followed by a set of linked stories that illustrate aspects of that issue, all of which build to a resolution—an answer to her question. For example, she begins one segment by asking "Why don't I tell stories about my childhood to my kids?" She then tells several stories: she loved stories as a child, especially because her dad changed the endings so she wouldn't be scared; she worked very hard to distance herself from childhood sexual abuse; she attended a conference at which she felt personally affirmed and got up the courage to work on her recovery by leaving home; she tried to protect herself against her stepfather, but her mother was not protective; her own son was sexually abused by one of her brothers; family events were essentially drunken brawls where the police would be called. And so she realizes that the reason she doesn't tell stories to her kids is because "there are no good stories to tell!"

The narrative form is a literary performance with dramatic expression in its presentation. I listened to the narratives carefully several times and parsed them based on auditory clues. I attempted to segment phrases the way the women did in the telling, and added pauses, intonation contours, changes in pace, word emphasis, gestures, sound effects, and other embellishments. I noted their vocabulary choices, syntax, rhetorical style, and connectors used for entrances and exits to their narrative segments. I found the women's narratives often fit into stanzas, sometimes accompanied by rhyme, repetition, and poetic rhythm.

Andi's utterances sound poetic in the way she repeats both words and phrases. In the following example, she describes a commander who was anti-female and self-absorbed. She repeats the thought three times, each time adding more words to the phrase until she ends with a complete sentence: "He was out for himself and not [pause] anybody else and didn't care about anybody else, okay? He really didn't care about anybody else [pause] in the unit."

Metaphors are basic linguistic tools that provide us with a semantic container to express abstract meanings in an imaginative, yet concrete, manner. Metaphoric expressions are a key to deeper cultural conceptions. I examined the narratives for prevailing metaphors and themes, particularly those of self-identity. Who the woman "really" was became less important than the symbolic image she created for herself. The idea was not simply to take the narrative at face value, but to search for the intersections between personal biographies and the collective culture. I coded interviews using the computer software program QSR Nud*ist 4 (Non-numerical Unstructured Data Indexing Searching and Theory-building—see Exercise Four). An example of a prevailing metaphor of self-identity comes from Betty. Her narrative was organized by geographic, tourist, and map metaphors. Betty told me, "There's no moss growing under my feet. I bounce with the wind." It seemed wherever Betty landed on her narrative map, a travel metaphor would creep in: "Because I'm the oldest, it's just a natural ride." "It just trips me out!" "I'm strictly a suitcase student." "I was able to get from point A to point B." "It's been a long time since I've been to Vegas [referring to the place where she had orthopedic surgery]."

I also studied the interactive components of the interviews because the narrative is not simply a text divorced from the situation in which it was generated. The veterans and I negotiated the sea of cultural performance and meanings until we found a wave that would carry us to a shore of understanding. An example that was prevalent in the narratives was the phrase, "you know?" This apparently meaningless filler actually expresses the thought that the narrator and the interviewer share some culture; using it is a way to bring the two together—either by reinforcing what the narrator assumes the interviewer should already know or by instructing her so that she is now an initiate into the narrator's world.

YOUR PROJECT

You may use the life history you produced in the course of completing the assignment for an earlier chapter or, if you prefer, you may use Lynn's narrative from my own research, excerpts of which are reproduced below. Complete Exercise One (see below) and as many of the other suggested exercises as you have time for or as your instructor chooses to assign. Please note my code system, which you may want to use in working with your own narrative, although you should feel free to devise one of your own:

[p] pause of 2–3 seconds
[P] pause of 4–5 seconds
[LP] long pause of 6–7 seconds
[VLP] very long pause or silence for more than 7 seconds
. . . indicates voice trails off
items in italics are words that were emphasized in speech
items underlined are words that were very strongly emphasized in speech
\\ indicates a slowing of pace or a lowering pitch of voice
// indicates a louder pitch or more animated voice tone
I refers to the Interviewer
[ ] indicates side comments, usually indicating emotional overtones or activities, such as [laughs] or [cries]; also used to indicate tone of voice, such as [angrily] or [in a monotone].

Note that the transcription is set out in separate phrases, which reflects the way Lynn, like most people, actually talks. Few people reel off complete, grammatically correct sentences in informal dialogue. In this transcription, periods mark points at which Lynn's voice drops, indicating that she has reached a conclusion, and a question mark indicates that her voice rises (even if what she is saying isn't strictly speaking a question); otherwise punctuation is kept to a minimum, as it would impose an order that is lacking in an informal verbal exchange.

LYNN'S NARRATIVE

(From my field notes: Lynn was vivacious, attractive, and extroverted. She laughed frequently with a carefree toss of her hair. Used gestures liberally, eye contact nearly continual. Interview conducted in a private room at her workplace. Lynn puzzles me because the cheerfulness and resilience she projects is unusual compared with others I've talked with.)

See, after being in [p] uh [P] the military . . .

This environment here [p] at the university is uh [p] is like . . .

I [p] call it a safe haven.

Because people are so protected here, you know? (I: uh huh)

In the military they want the *image* [p] that everyone is the <u>same</u> [p] you know? (I: oh, okay)

That's why [switches from animated to monotone] they make you cut your hair [p] the same

That's the way they make the uniforms all l-look alike

It's to help p-promote [p] uh [p] espirit de corps—teamwork, you know? (I: Ahh)

You're just one piece of a working *machine*, you know? (I: uh huh)

Your individuality doesn't <u>count</u> [P] um [P] as much as [VLP] your presence to make a *whole*, you know?

I mean it's not like . . . (I: And they let you know that real *clearly*)

[animated] Oh! That's their *whole*—that's a [p] *basic* part of their *philosophy*.

Quality management won't *work* in certain aspects of the military

You can't have [p] you can't have [p] somebody [p] in the *army*

Be told to go out there on the front <u>line</u>

And say, "Wait, you know! I think we should *talk* about this—I might have a *better* idea!" [chuckles]

It doesn't *work*! (I: Right!)

You know, the person has to go out there [p] they've signed an agreement

They've given *up* their constitutional rights

They have their rights under the Uniformed Code of Military Justice (I: justice)

It's not the same.

You don't have freedom of speech

You don't have freedom of the press

You don't have . . . [P] because you have to keep some things confidential

You have to . . . [p] you're not allowed to say certain things

You're not allowed to *write* certain things . . .

And that can't *happen* in the civilian world

(Continues to describe differences between civilian and military life, and contrasts the latter with her present work environment, which she says is like "dying and going to Heaven," but hastens to add:)

I *loved* the military [P] I loved every minute of it!

I retired from the military, so [p]

(I: You *did!* [surprised because Lynn is so young]. So you got a whole career. Oh, I gotta hear everything!)

[monotone, like a recitation] You know, I was one of the first girls [p] in my career field

I was the first girl [p] that ever [P] did my job at the first base I went to

And . . . you know, it wasn't really welcome there

(Describes her opinion of sexual harassment, giving examples of how some of her colleagues handled certain situations. Thinks sexual harassment is based on childlike curiosity or resistance to change, and is a contest that you learn how to handle at a young age as a social skill.)

But I've had a great life!

(I: Yes, *tell* me about [p] your life—usually I just say [p] ask you to explain how you got from when you were tiny to where you are *now* in your life)

[monotone] \\ Okay—um [P] wonderful childhood [p] magical [p] (I: In what way?)

Nothing bad [P] uh [p] Mom and Dad [P] loving, good [p] no bad stuff

Uh [p] no abuse in the family. . . (I: No dysfunction?)

// [laughs] No! (I: Wow! The one in a million?) [both laugh]

I was the dysfunctional one [p] if there was *any*, you know? [both laugh again]

Um [p] I had a brother who was really, really smart [p]

Never got into trouble unless maybe staying up too late [p] *reading* [laughs]

That would be *it!*

[monotone] \\ Then there was me [P] I was always a tomboy growing up

I was always, you know [p] into something

I was always causing [P] always coming up with something [p] Mom and Dad weren't prepared for . . .

(Describes a childhood incident where she was sexually abused by a babysitter, though she did not recognize it as abuse until later. Thinks the boy was only curious, but admits she found it "scary" when he threatened if she told on him, something "bad" would happen, since Lynn had never had any "bad's gonna happen" in her life before.)

I [p] in my life [p] I've been // *raped* before

And I've been [p] um [P] \\ date-raped type thing before

Um [P] one was totally innocent on my part

Um, just jogging in my neighborhood

Before I joined the Air Force

Somebody came up from behind me [p] asked me for directions

// It was <u>midnight</u> [p] I probably had no *reason* [p] but I never had a reason <u>not</u> to jog at midnight

I was getting ready to go to basic training, you know

And I—I couldn't sleep, I was excited

\\ I'd go out and practice running

And somebody came up to me and put a knife to my throat

And pulled my tee-shirt up over my head

And said they were gonna kill me [p] and the whole nine yards

And it was really scary (I: Yeah!)

And I was living by myself at the time . . .

// But [p] um [P] I *lived through* it (I: um hum)

[small laugh] I don't have any [P] <u>scars</u>, you know

Nothing—he didn't—he *didn't* hurt me

I [p] for somehow [P] remembered a bunch of <u>scripture</u>!

And started [laughs] reciting it [laughs] (I: Wow! How interesting!)

And yeah, and *yeah* [laughs]

And he was like, "*This* is too *much!*"

And let me go (I: That's too much! Like thought you were talking in tongues!)

I couldn't *believe* it! (I: *Really!* What a strategy!)

I guess it's like [p] good thing he believed in <u>God</u>, you know? [both laugh]

You know, I was *lucky*, I was <u>lucky</u> (I: Strange, huh?)

Yeah, I got away after—and [p] I mean, he <u>did</u> what he was gonna *do*

[spoken rapidly] But he didn't cut me up in little pieces and leave me in the *bushes* like he said

So *hey!* I felt like I was a <u>winner</u>!

Now some people might have felt like a <u>victim</u> after that

But I felt like a *survivor* after that (I: What's the difference, do you think? I'm always so curious about the difference in that perception.)

[P] I don't know [LP] I was [P]

I <u>think</u> [p] it's because I felt more [p] <u>clever</u> than he was

Like I convinced him not to *hurt* me any more [p] and to let me go and leave!

And maybe that was his intention all the time [P] and maybe he never *meant* to hurt me [p] or kill me

But I felt like I <u>won</u> that battle . . .

(Lynn discusses mild residual effects. If someone comes up behind her, her heart will race, for example.)

Ummm [p] let's see [p] when I was in the military though

After basic training [P] I was in a \\ coed flight [P] and drum and bugle

Had [p] uh [p] 10 girls and 42 guys [p] in our flight

And [p] uh [p] // let me tell you what

That was about as *easy* of a basic training as you could have [chuckles]

We had two guys [p] um [p] training instructors

And they couldn't come into the barracks [P] because we were girls

Until a certain time (I: So they couldn't inspect?)

Well [p] not during the *night*—you know, they couldn't come in at night,

And we would have like [p] little [p] *slumber* parties [p] and stuff [laughs]

And like, it wasn't like other people have in the military (I: Sounds like camp!)

I <u>mean</u>, so all my time [P] I've had *good* parts, you know [p] I've had bad things happen to me,

But I've had [slows pace for emphasis] // a really *good, lucky, lucky* life,

You know what I mean? (I: uh huh)

I've always had it extra easy [p] than most people

So maybe when bad things happen [p] maybe I can handle it a little better, I don't know.

Um, now [p] I [p] I have been irresponsible at times

And drank too much?

And in one situation when I was in technical school?

When I was in technical school?

And we were doing one of these drinking games, you know (I: Yeah? Oh no!)

It was called Cardinal Puff [p] is what it was called

And you'd have to recite this long [p] um [P] verb [P] verbiage thing,

This whole long big [p] like recited thing

And if you didn't say it right and [p] tap your knee three times [p] or something

Then every time you messed up [p] you had to take a drink.

// And I got plowed [p] *Plowed*! <u>Plowed</u>! (I: Aw!)

And it was a bunch of *really* dear friends of mine that I'd made

And [P] the guys carried me [p] to my room [P]

And they put me to bed [P] and they locked me in there

And they laid me on my stomach [p] in case I got sick, you know?

So I wouldn't kill myself in my sleep (I: uh huh)

And [p] um [P] there was this *guy* [p] who'd been threatening the girl next door

Saying, [p] "*I've* got a master key [p] I'm gonna come in your room and *get* ya one night"

Well he saw them carrying me into my room

\\ And [p] um [P] when I woke up [P] I woke up and there was somebody in my room

And he was on top of me [p] the whole nine yards

// And I was *sick* [P] I was <u>so</u> sick [p] I was like throwing up

I woke up, I [p] I'd thrown up in my *hair*!

I mean, I *wasn't* gonna go to the hospital without taking a <u>shower</u>!

You know, *no*! [laughs]

So I went to the hospital after I'd taken a shower and made the report

The guys in the [p] in the dorm and the girl next door

They all [P] gave [p] statements, saying that,

You know, this guy said that I'd asked him in and opened the door for him [chuckle]

[laughing] And they were like, "There's *no way!*

She was passed out *cold* [laughs] you know, this and that"

And they said that [p] he had held up the key [p] and flashed it

And threatened this other girl [p] and that's how he got in the room

And you know, the bad part about the military

I was at this point [p] *ashamed*

Because it was my fault this time [P] because I'd let myself get so [p] drunk [P] that (I: but . . .)

Well, it's *still* wrong what he *did*, but I felt ashamed [p] that time,

'Cause I had some control over it [p] had I been more [p] alert. (I: So you felt had you not let yourself be vulnerable by getting drunk . . .)

Right. So um [P] but they said

In the military—then it was [p] 1978

And he told [P] and I was told it would be handled

That this guy would be taken care of and it would be handled . . .

(Lynn explains that she assumed the guy would be in big trouble but instead, she and all those who made statements on her behalf were kicked out of the privileged drum and bugle corps and sent back to their regular squadrons for technical training.)

We got punished [P] *we* got punished [p] for it. (I: And him?)

Uh [p] I don't know [p] all I know is that he got stationed somewhere else

And later on [P] before I left that base [P] in a Commander's Call? (I: uh hum)

They were making jokes about some girl [p] who'd claimed that some guy'd come into her room [embarrassed laugh]

And I was just *appalled!* [p] I was just appalled (I: [murmur of sympathy])

I was never invited [p] or privileged to any information as to what *happened to him*, where he *went*—anything.

So it was just that good ole boys' network, you know (I: protecting him)

So it wasn't just *my* word against his [p] you know?

It was a whole group of people's word [p] against his

And it was just [p] brushed under the table [p] and we were all punished [p] and [P]

And this other guy was just sent off somewhere else to another base—and another job

He was sent off that base (I: uh huh)

But that was all [P] that ever happened to him [P] you know?

And he'd *hurt* one girl—me [P] and he'd *threatened* another

And that's all that ever happened to him [P] to my knowledge. (I: That's not right. But I've heard that . . .

Yeah, so that's my bad story [P] that's my bad story.

But on the other hand, there was a real nice chaplain?

That talked to me [p] he made me hot chocolate [slight laugh] and he talked to me that next whole day

And he made things really, really easy for me . . .

I was never given a report [P] never given any follow-up action, you know?

And it was a *crime* I reported. (I: That's right!)

But I never even got, "Ahh, you're crazy"

I never even got [p] even if you report a crime and [P] you lose

Somebody *still* lets you know [P] and they didn't ever let me know

And that was my [P] biggest disappointment the whole time I was in the military

They let me down there

The *rest* of the time [P] I was as *proud* as could be [P] to be [laughs] to be in the Air Force!

And that was in the very beginning [P] and I just blew that off

I figured, well [P] I'll probably mess up myself once or twice every now and then.

I'll give you a mistake in the beginning [chuckles] if you'll give me a mistake later on, you know?

That was my internal way of dealing with it, you know? (I: Nice that you're gentle with yourself)

I just, um—I'm [p] really proud to be an [p] American? (I: uh hum)

I'm really *proud* [p] to be a Floridian? (I: uh hum)

And I'm not gonna let something like *that*

Take away a lifetime of belief [p] in a system, or a culture or [p] anything like that.

You know, I know that even though it might have been [P] institutional type of [p] um, um

What do you call that? Discrimination? (I: uh huh) You know, the systematic—the way it was set up?

It was still [P] applied by individuals [p] you know what I mean?

That decided among themselves individually [P] that it might not be important enough to pursue

It wasn't like the Secretary of the Air Force or anybody else

So I don't hold it against the Air Force . . .

(Lynn then talks about how she gave up a golf scholarship to join the Air Force and kept re-enlisting because she was enjoying herself.)

When you're in the military [P] you're all transplanted [p] and moved around from one place to another

And that [p] in itself [p] besides your basic training that you all become familiar with

And have that under your belt [p] your training in your specialty [p] you have *that* in common

But you also have that common bond of being transplanted and displaced. (I: Ah, that's right.)

So that helps build com [p] camaraderie

Well [p] with people you never probably would have made *friends* with any other way

You *know?* (I: 'Cause you're thrown together and there's no one else?)

// Yeah, you know [P] you're hanging out with somebody and they're from Nebraska,

Not because they wanted to move to *Florida*

But because they got stationed here [p] whether they *like* it or <u>not</u> [both laugh]

You know? Those are the only people I think [p] are allowed to complain about the *weather!*

For the most part [p] they were all like big brothers [p] they were *nice!*

You know, they helped me *move* [P] they helped me [P] *shop,*

They helped me fix my *car* [P] they helped me *buy* my car,

I mean, it was like a *family!*

And I miss it [P] today, but [p] // don't think I wasn't ready to get out when I was able to get a *pension* for the rest of my life!

But, you know, I loved it . . .

(Discusses her opinion of Clinton affair and ole boys' club in the military. Describes her work on flight simulators, then talks about foot accident and how military surgeons were able to save her foot from an amputation. Tells next of being dumped three weeks before her wedding. Then describes her home that her uncle financed, her car that was a gift from her parents, her pension, and her great health benefits.)

See, we're talking storybook life!

(She describes her childhood and how her parents and grandparents were always there for her.)

They never had those roles—those traditional roles where the mom stayed home? (I: yeah)

The men in my family always cooked and did the dishes. (I: So [p] no traditional expectations for you to like go into nursing or be a schoolteacher!)

No [p] nope [P] my dad was Marine in World War II (I: Oh wow)

So I didn't have any exposure to that!

You know, but, ah, he was saying [P] you know [P] you could be a Marine

Yes you can [p] *girls* can be Marines too.

I'd go, "*Harumph!*" [p] you know, that kind of thing . . . they never . . .

(Talks lovingly and describes more about her family and her feeling of security.)

I always had security [P] I never felt insecure

I never felt insecure in the military [p] and now that I'm retired [p] I still have that security

And now [p] I have the security of another [p] government job (I: oh yeah)

I'm *big* on security! [laughs] I'm big on security . . .

I don't like the ability of anyone to be able [P] to take anything away from me

So I don't [p] give anybody that ability [p] or that power [p] to take anything away from me

And I think now that's why I'm single, you know? (I: uh huh)

Because I don't think I'd want anybody to . . .

The way I look at it, I've had people die to get me what I have

And that was very devastating and it was [P] that shook me up.

If I've ever had a loss in my entire life

That would have been the death of my uncle [p] he was very close to me

(Describes her close relationship with her uncle and how she was with him and held him when he died.)

I had [P] I have a dreamy life when it comes to that!

Yeah [P] I might have been abused or harassed by outside [p] entities

By people that aren't really [p] of my world, but

They didn't—they didn't hurt my world.

They might have caused me some disappointment [p] in a system

Or disappointment [p] in some people

Or [p] even disappointment [p] in myself here or there

But nothing that couldn't have been improved or remedied or [P]

You haven't met very many people as lucky as me, have you? (I: No)

I don't mind to claim it either

You know, I know people [P] I know people [P] I know women [p] that have been raped [p] not *even* as bad or as scarily as I was, okay?

That [p] to this day [P] are haunted by it [P] they let it consume their *whole* life.

Now do you *really* [p] want to give that situation *that* much power?

Do you want to give that guy that did that to you that much power? That much credit?

Now [P] I let my uncle's *death* devastate me

And I say I let it devastate me [P] because that's the only way it could [p] devastate me

You know, I was glad [p] I was there for him

But you see, I *loved* him [P] and he was a very big part of my world

So he's allowed to devastate me!

A stranger [p] or somebody who doesn't like [p] who I don't like

Or who I don't know [p] I don't let devastate me [laugh]

They don't get that far [P] that's the way I look at it

I don't let them devastate me . . .

(Tells a long story about a friend who lost a leg and who was an inspiration to her. Describes how she gets her philosophy from the way her mother and father have dealt with cancer and Parkinson's respectively.)

You can feel [p] anyway you want to about something

Just like vanilla and chocolate [P] everybody loves [p] *both* of 'em [laughs], you know?

You know, you just gotta look at how you like it, you know?

Like what's right for you [P] so that's the way I look at that

You can't let things get to you [P] there's always a brighter day
You can let yourself laugh
You get through it—you get well. (I: I hear a lot of gratitude—I've heard that since I sat down! And looking on the good side. Definitely a glass-half-full person, huh? Or ¾?)
Yeah, yeah, I'm not [P] I've got plenty!
Yeah, I don't need it full [p] but as long as I don't get thirsty! [both laugh]
My glass is full enough [P] I never really never wanted to be [p] rich
I've got everything I need [p] I have a good life
I'm very happy [P] I'm very content.

EXERCISE ONE: FIELD NOTES AND MEMOS

Write a "field note" highlighting your initial impressions. Narratives are interpretations and are not meant to mirror some reality that is "out there." Narrative analysis is about searching for meanings that are constructed out of the interaction of the interviewer and the narrator. Value your own interpretations as a starting point. You may be surprised to discover some of your own cultural preconceptions in the process. Some questions you might ask yourself: How do this narrator's conceptions differ from my own? Does this narrator reflect what can be called "culturally prescribed" behaviors? What beliefs of the narrator can I identify from the narrative? What did I learn about the person's cultural setting? Does the narrator fit my idea of a stereotypical member of the group to which s/he belongs? Which setting, stage props, major characters, and script or storyline have been selected by the narrator? Does the personal narrative correspond with any collective cultural values? What questions would I ask this narrator now if I had the opportunity?

EXERCISE TWO: STRUCTURE AND FUNCTION

Take a large sheet of drawing paper and some colored pencils and enlist your creative imagination. Draw the narrator's plot in any shape or form you think fits. Try to depict patterns within the narrator's personal story. How does s/he treat the disruptions that occur in life and explain them so that they form a coherent pattern? How does s/he glue the discordant pieces of life together into a concordant whole? Can you identify an overarching theme in the narrator's account? What title would you give the narrative?

EXERCISE THREE: DRAMATIC PRESENTATION

Examine the narrative for literary performance. Try to find examples of the following: repetition, pauses, poetic stanzas, pace changes, voice pitch changes, word emphasis, vocabulary choices. Does the speaker use rapid, staccato-like speech, a conversational style, or a prepared recitation? Does s/he speak in short phrases or long, convoluted sentences? How frequently does the narrator use conversational fillers like "um" and "uh"? Address dramatic expression in the narrative: does the narrator take time to set up the story or plunge right in? Where does the narrator enhance details? Is the narrative organized or scrambled in terms of time, location, and theme? What verb tense does the narrator use? Do you sense that the person is exhibiting restraint or purposely avoiding certain topics? Does the narrator present the story from an abstract or a concrete orientation?

EXERCISE FOUR: METAPHORS AND THEMES

For this exercise you may try using QSR Nud*ist or another qualitative research software tool. Programs like Nud*ist are ideal for detailed dissection of content because they assist in indexing and coding large amounts of data. But even if you use such software, go over the data with the old-fashioned "ear and eyeball" method so as to identify the larger elements of trajectory, shape, and literary performance. With Nud*ist you can set up cross-referencing networks and jump back to the original document within seconds, or print out a coding summary report that includes the links and excerpts from your original documents. There are "find and display" capabilities for text searching; you may, for example, want to count the number of times a certain word is used. In Nud*ist you create your own custom coding system by assigning your data to what the program calls "nodes." These nodes are flexible and can also be layered as an outline.

If you do not have access to such software, you may use Microsoft Word and split the screen using the document-map icon. Doing so brings up a separate pane, and each category you identify can be set as a first-, second-, or third-level outline heading, which allows you to rapidly navigate through the document to code without losing your place. Don't forget to include your own memos, diary, or field notes in your textual analysis.

In this exercise, you will categorize symbols and metaphors you find in the narrative. What do you see that reflects the narrator's conceptual system? What original imagery can you find? Can you identify recurring themes or symbols? Look for a pattern of personal myth (a consistent way in which the narrator symbolizes him/herself), which may be stated outright or merely implied. Some themes might include betrayal, life-death contrasts, freedom, romance, adventure, and so forth.

EXERCISE FIVE: ANALYSIS OF INTERACTIONS

Examine the narrative as an interactive document. Write a paragraph about the exchanges between the narrator and the interviewer. What insight does their exchange give you about the larger cultural context? Note how the script can change depending on the audience. For example, how might the narrator tell the story differently to an aunt or uncle, as opposed to a close friend or to a researcher from the university? What factors influence which version a person selects to suit different types of situations? Can you find instances where the interaction itself changes the momentum in the narrative encounter?

A FEW SELECTED READINGS FOR FURTHER INFORMATION

Angrosino, Michael V. 1989. *Documents of Interaction: Biography, Autobiography, and Life History in Social Science Perspective.* Gainesville: University of Florida Press.

Becker, Gay. 1997. *Disrupted Lives: How People Create Meaning in a Chaotic World.* Berkeley: University of California Press.

Gee, James P. Units in the Production of Narrative Discourse. *Discourse Processes* 9:391–422.

Janesick, Valerie J. 1994. The Dance of Qualitative Research Design. In *Handbook of Qualitative Research*, ed. Norman K. Denzin and Yvonna S. Lincoln, 209–219. Thousand Oaks, CA: Sage.

Lakoff, George, and Mark Johnson. 1980. *Metaphors We Live By.* Chicago: University of Chicago Press.

Riessman, Catherine K. 1993. *Narrative Analysis.* Newbury Park, CA: Sage.

5

Reconstructing a Community through Archival Research

Cheryl Rodriguez & Yvette Baber

A RESEARCH PROJECT

Urban renewal has impacted African-American business enclaves in some typical and predictable ways. In the 1930s and 1940s such communities served as the hubs of commercial, political, and cultural activity, but by the mid-1950s they were experiencing a rapid decline. Various forces, including neglect by city government, dramatic social changes resulting from the civil-rights movement, and construction of interstate highways, all contributed to the despair that eroded the economic and cultural foundations of such communities, which came to be identified as pockets of poverty, crime, and ongoing racial unrest. By the 1960s the planned destruction and demolition of the communities were well underway despite protests from loosely organized groups of concerned citizens. By the late 1970s formerly thriving and vibrant communities were leveled and gone, often with no marker or sign to acknowledge their former importance and no formal or organized documentation of the beliefs, achievements, and histories of those who lived and worked there. Virtually every major American city has seen a variant of this basic scenario, which must be pieced together from oral narratives, scattered magazine or newspaper articles, dusty photographs, and public records.

It is true that the stories of most of the demolished African-American communities have a basic similarity. Nevertheless, the distinctive history of each community has value for those who once frequented the place, whose heritage is all too often misrepresented, or ignored altogether, in historical accounts of the city. Negative images of the community's declining years loom large in the minds of those who choose to remember only the trouble brought on by dispirited residents. Other members of the larger community are too young to recollect images of the lost community as a thriving refuge for black people from all walks of life. Public anthropology, in the form of community heritage projects, can illuminate, revive, and reconstruct these lost histories. As members of communities, urban anthropologists can make significant and substantive contributions to local knowledge by recapturing images of hope, self-determination, agency, and strength. Such was our goal in the early 1990s when we became involved with the Central Avenue project, a commemoration and celebration of African-American history in Tampa, Florida. Several ethnographic data-collection techniques were used to reconstruct this lost history, but the collection and analysis of archival data played a key role in the project. The official title of the project was "Central Avenue Legacies: Commerce and Community in Tampa's African American History," and it was initiated by faculty and students in the departments of Anthropology and Africana Studies at the University of South Florida (USF) The researchers were supported by an advisory committee composed of local residents and city employees.

ARCHIVAL RESEARCH AS A TOOL OF ETHNOGRAPHIC RESEARCH

Archival data are qualitative and quantitative materials stored for research, service, and other official and unofficial purposes by researchers, service organizations, and other groups. The data are stored in the formats in which they were collected, although sometimes they have been transformed into computer-readable formats.

Archival data properly speaking are materials originally collected for bureaucratic or administrative purposes that are transformed into data for research purposes. Examples include: maps that can identify physical features and structures in communities and neighborhoods; municipal records of births, marriages, real-estate transactions, and property ownership; census, tax, and voting lists; specialized surveys; service system records from human service organizations; court proceedings; minutes of meetings of local groups. Also useful are "secondary data," raw data that other researchers collected for their own purposes but that can be analyzed for other purposes; it is sometimes possible, for example, to access the personal field notes of prior researchers, or to use formal ethnographic databases such as the *Atlas of World Cultures* or the Human Relations Area Files. Local secondary data, material collected in the community under study, are particularly valuable, although secondary data obtained from related research conducted elsewhere on related topics or similar populations are also important sources.

Archival research has a number of advantages that enhance qualitative research. It is non-reactive (i.e., the researcher does not influence people's responses, since he/she is not interacting directly with those providing the information). It is relatively inexpensive. It supports the study of cultural processes through time. And it is possible to study topics that might be too politically or socially controversial to study firsthand. Moreover, the use of data from archival and secondary sources can also enhance the comprehensiveness of data collection by allowing for cross-cultural and cross-national comparability and generalizability. On the other hand, archival data cannot always be considered "clean" or unbiased, nor can they be used without due consideration for the ways in which the information was stored and coded. The standards of documentation that we expect today were not always observed in the past. Even modern statistical databases, which may seem ideally bias-free (especially if they come from data banks and are already packaged on computer tape, coded and ready to be analyzed) can still be riddled with errors. It is important to consider carefully all the possible sources of bias that can be at work in the setting down of the data. Archival data are not always stored in ways that support ease of retrieval. They may be in filing cabinets or folders, and the researcher may have to organize and code the material manually. Since doing so can be very time-consuming, it is a good idea to make an early decision about which data are most important to your study.

ARCHIVAL RESEARCH: THE PROCESS

In the 1890s the largest segment of the black[1] population in Tampa was located in an area called the Scrub. This community, which had been settled by freed slaves, was neglected, undeveloped, and poverty-ridden. Clapboard shacks and makeshift dwellings leaned precariously and haphazardly along unpaved neighborhood streets. Despite its squalor, however, the Scrub had the advantage of being located close to the shipping docks and railroads, important sources of employment, particularly for African-American men. As Tampa's citrus, cigar, and phosphate industries flourished, African Americans migrated to the area in large numbers.

In the 1880s and 1890s, black barbers, seamstresses, and bootmakers had shops in downtown Tampa, where they served a predominantly white clientele. As Tampa's African-American population grew in the Scrub and surrounding neighborhoods, the passage of Jim Crow laws dictated segregation of public facilities, schools, and businesses. The black business owners were strongly encouraged to leave downtown and operate in specially designated areas of the city. Central Avenue, which bordered the Scrub, was very close to downtown and it became a prime location for the development of black businesses. In 1893 there were five black-owned businesses on Central, including a barber shop, a restaurant, and two grocery stores. In 1899 there were more than twenty-eight businesses, and by 1918 more than eighty shops, stores, and professional offices had been developed to serve Tampa's black residents. Central Avenue became more than just buildings and services. In the 1920s the election of a "mayor" of Central Avenue became an annual fund-raising event. A tradition of parades began in response to the exclusion of blacks from major civic festivities elsewhere in Tampa. One such parade, the "Tilt of the Maroon and Gold," was held during an annual football rivalry between two historically black colleges—Florida A&M University and Bethune-Cookman College.

During its heyday in the 1940s and 1950s, Central Avenue thrived as the "main drag," the functional equivalent to downtown for the city's black population. It was a site of black entertainment known throughout Florida, and nationally renowned artists such as Cab Calloway, B. B. King, and Ray Charles all performed in Central Avenue night clubs early in their careers. Black entertainers, however, like all other black travelers, had limited access to public accommodations in Tampa. The Central Hotel provided shelter and community for these entertainers as well as for other black visitors. Aside from entertainment venues, there were social clubs, fraternal organizations, burial societies, church groups, and literary clubs. These groups worked together to create libraries, day-care centers, scholarship funds, and other responses to community emergencies. The black community's first newspaper, which still thrives, was published and delivered on Central. These events and activities fostered solidarity among African Americans and defined the Central Avenue community as one that could create and sustain itself.

There was a strong tradition of activism in the community as well, and it was a center for the continuing fight for civil rights. Tampa's Urban League, the National Association for the Advancement of Colored People (NAACP), and the Longshoremen's Union were all located in the Central Avenue community. Tampa's first black law firm began on Central, and its lead attorney became the chief legal counsel for the NAACP. Many of the major discrimination lawsuits filed in Tampa and in the state of Florida were initiated by this firm. Civil-rights leaders from all over the U.S. met at the St. Paul AME Church (which continues to have an active congregation) to plan sit-ins and demonstrations that eventually facilitated the dismantling of Jim Crow laws in Tampa.

Despite this rich history of self-determination and entrepreneurship, the Central Avenue business district began to falter in the 1960s. Some people blame desegregation for its loss, while some attribute the decline to a riot or civil disturbance on Central Avenue in 1967. Others argue that racial discrimination blocked black business owners' access to loans that would have supported the revitalization of the area. In any case, by 1974 Central Avenue's demise was finalized with wrecking balls and bulldozers. The 387 multi-storied structures of the community were reduced to rubble in a matter of days, although the plans to demolish the businesses had been in the works for years. In 1973 the mayor of Tampa announced a $4.7 million HUD grant to level the buildings and replace them with a park named in honor of a local African-American community leader. Today there are no physical reminders of a bustling economic enclave. The street itself became Orange Avenue, a nondescript, half-mile thoroughfare leading to Interstates 4 and 75. Beyond the sidewalk that borders Orange Avenue is Perry Harvey, Sr. Park, where children from the Central Park Village public-housing complex play. The only structures remaining from the days of Central Avenue are the Longshoremen's Hall and Kid Mason Center, a recreational facility operated by the city of Tampa. These buildings, along with two churches in the immediate area, are historic, but even today their survival remains uncertain as redevelopment continues to threaten the area.

The final products of the USF researchers' efforts and the planning of the community advisory committee were a photo exhibit, a panel discussion, and a walking tour of the area that once had been Central Avenue. The photo exhibit and discussion were based at Kid Mason Center, and the walking tour was facilitated through a series of exhibits erected in the park and standing on the sites of bygone businesses. The exhibits were doors collected from junkyards, and each one represented an address of a former business. Photographs and other memorabilia associated with the businesses were displayed on the doors. The walking tours were led by a police officer who had once walked the Central Avenue beat and by an older resident who had worked on Central Avenue.

Despite the overwhelming success of the day-long community program, our tasks in developing this public heritage project were many and complex. Some of the challenges faced in the course of research were the result of the mere fact that the businesses and residences had been destroyed. Moreover, many potential informants were either deceased or elderly with failing memories. The research team also had to organize and catalog materials and artifacts including personal photos (with questionable dates), unannotated newspaper clippings, and interview transcripts (with accompanying tapes) from a study of Tampa's African-American community conducted in the 1970s. The transcripts and tapes represented the only remaining evidence of the early lives of seventy of Tampa's African-American residents. While photographs from the *Florida Sentinel-Bulletin*, the local African-American newspaper, were critical to the project, they were not filed in a way that made for ease of access. We often had to go through the storage boxes one picture at a time.

Our research was designed to document the impact of federal, state, and local urban renewal policy on the Central Avenue neighborhood. We were interested in the ways in which community members responded to the impending destruction of their neighborhood. We were particularly concerned about confirming or refuting the widespread story that "riots" had precipitated the demise of the neighborhood. It was also important for us to understand which individuals or entities benefited most from the demise of Central Avenue and to learn about the impact of the destruction on the African-American community in Tampa. In order to achieve these research aims, we attempted to construct a longitudinal review of property ownership in the area using a combination of archival resources, ethnographic interviews, personal materials from key informants, and content analysis of local newspapers.

An important first step in archival research is to identify the data you will be retrieving. You will need support in this process from the offices, institutions, or individuals who are in possession of the information. You must therefore learn who controls access to the data and then identify and carry out formal and informal procedures for gaining access to the data. The formal procedures may include paperwork, and it is important to understand the informal relationships and "chain-of-command" issues that could facilitate (or slow down) your research. It is almost always necessary to obtain informed consent if the data describe individual cases. If you are borrowing valuable personal items (e.g., photos or other mementos), be sure to work out a plan to protect them while they are in your custody and to return them safely to their owners at the conclusion of the project. Even before accessing the data, you should develop a means for recording and/or copying them. Technological advances have simplified this process, but it is important to consider the costs of copying materials that you cannot take away with you.

Researchers need to make decisions about how much time to spend collecting the data based on availability and storage methods. Do not forget to factor in the time it takes to secure necessary permission to access the information. You should also consider the amount of staff cooperation you will need—such people are likely to be very busy and will not be enthusiastic about helping with your project if they think they will end up spending lots of time on your agenda. If it seems that you will be able to access a large quantity of information, you may want to think about whether all of it needs to be collected, or if only a sample will suffice.

Before collecting data, create a way to record it. Your recording system should identify the source of information, the dates, and the location of the files (or other sources). Always allow space for comments. A database file (e.g., Microsoft Access or FileMaker Pro) may serve this purpose, as might a conventional spreadsheet. You will then be able to sort information by date, location, and other pertinent indices.

YOUR PROJECT

In most localities, both urban and rural, there are areas that have a long history of settlement, often by people of a common ethnic, racial, or family background. Over the years, however, such areas may undergo changes in occupancy, in socioeconomic status, or in land use as a result of governmental policies related to development.

Your assignment is to trace the history of such a neighborhood in your locality, documenting its founding and any significant changes it has undergone over time. Using archival resources such as residential directories, newspapers, maps, and minutes of meetings of public bodies such as city councils or county commissions, you will identify the historical trajectory that led to the neighborhood's change; analyze the impact of federal, state, and local policies on neighborhood change; describe changes in the neighborhood's economic base, the ethnic/racial make-up of the residents over time, and the social institutions of the neighborhood; become familiar with the process of accessing and interpreting data at the city, county, state, and federal levels; and understand the importance of paper, microform, and electronic media resources in providing contextual descriptions of neighborhood change.

This project is best conducted as a team. Break up the tasks among members of the team, assigning one source per person. It is important, however, to share the fruits of individual research so that everyone on the team has at least a basic familiarity with all the sources and the kinds of data to be used. Everyone should agree on a recording/coding system and use it consistently.

Your final report should include a historical time line or table that highlights key events that shaped the area under study. It may be that each member of the team comes up with his/her own time line based on the particular data source he/she worked with. But all the team members should pool their tables into one common time line.

The report should describe the origins, history, and current status of the community under study. What is its heritage? How was it founded? What have been the major influences for change over time (e.g., economic factors, race, social class)? What has happened to the original residents? What does the area look like now? Are there plans (or policies) in place that may bring about further change in the area? Be sure to include your own personal observations about the process and about the neighborhood you are learning about.

NOTE

[1] In this chapter we use the terms "African-American" and "black" interchangeably. Please note, however, that in other contexts, the former term is often restricted to people of African heritage whose family history has been in the United States, while the latter refers to others of the "African diaspora" whose family histories are in Cuba, the Bahamas, Jamaica, and other parts of the Caribbean. Even if they later came to the U.S., they often maintained their own distinctive cultural and national identities.

A FEW SELECTED READINGS FOR FURTHER INFORMATION

Bernard, H. Russell. 1988. *Research Methods in Cultural Anthropology.* Newbury Park, CA: Sage.

Butler, John Sibley. 1991. *Entrepreneurship and Self-Help among Black Americans.* Albany: State University of New York Press.

Greenbaum, Susan, and Cheryl Rodriguez. 1998. Central Avenue Legacies. *Practicing Anthropology* 20(1):2–30.

Lewis, Earl. 1996. Connecting Memory, Self, and the Power of Place in African American Urban History. In *The New African American Urban History,* ed. Kenneth W. Goings and Raymond A. Mohl, 1–15. Thousand Oaks, CA: Sage.

Schensul, Stephen L., Jean J. Schensul, and Margaret LeCompte. 1999. *Essential Ethnographic Methods: Observations, Interviews, and Questionnaires.* Walnut Creek, CA: AltaMira.

6

Using a Museum as a Resource for Ethnographic Research

Serena Nanda

Visiting a Museum while Conducting an Ethnographic Research Project

Proper viewing of museum exhibits draws on and reinforces many ethnographic skills. Because of their visual focus, museums utilize and improve observational skills, forcing us to pay attention to details and to the relationship of those details to the whole—a perspective that is at the heart of good ethnographic research. Absorbing ethnographic data from museum exhibits also improves note-taking skills; we can certainly copy information directly from exhibit labels, but we also need to organize our own thoughts about what is important about an object in relation to our particular research interests. In requiring analysis of both individual objects and of objects in rela-

71

tion to each other, museum exhibits also foster critical thinking and ethnographic theory-building.

A display of material culture is only the tip of the information iceberg available in museums, most of which today have libraries, websites, catalogues, brochures, photographic and audio archives, material in CD-ROM format, educational centers (for teachers, families, and children), film libraries, lectures, seminar series, cultural performances and demonstrations, and tours by competent guides (docents). Any or all of these services can help an ethnographer locate and make sense of information pertinent to a particular research project.

A visit to a museum can even help clarify general interests into a workable research project. Individuals respond differently to different objects, and without knowing much about any of the objects on display in a museum, you may nevertheless find yourself attracted by certain items or styles. My own favorites include wooden hats from the Northwest Coast of North America; gold weights from Asante, Ghana; feathered mantles from South American Amazonian societies; Hopi kachina dolls; Islamic calligraphy; and photographs of African-American life in Harlem in the 1920s. There is literally no end to the material collected in museums. There is a museum of rock 'n' roll in Cleveland and an exhibition of hip-hop culture ("Hip-Hop Nation: Roots, Rhymes and Rage") featuring rappers' sneakers at the Brooklyn Museum. One of the Guggenheim Museum's most popular recent shows was an exhibit of motorcycles. A good place to begin focusing a research project is to see which objects, items, or themes really capture your imagination; a compelling interest is the mainstay of any extended ethnographic project.

Such apparently aimless wandering through a museum led to my current ethnographic research project. I was visiting the ethnographic collections in the African room of the American Museum of Natural History and was intrigued by a carving of a slave ship with an Englishman in the bow. I began to pay closer attention to other museum exhibits and collections of objects from non-European cultures that represented Europeans. As often happens, once you get an idea and know what you are looking for, information begins to pile up. So I began scouring collections with a more focused eye, and found many objects that were relevant for my project. Of course, the very richness of museum exhibits, while awesome and inspiring, can also be overwhelming. Too much wandering around can result in sensory overload. I therefore believe that you will find a museum most useful in your ethnographic research if you already have at least some idea of a subject in mind, even if it is only vaguely formulated. You can then begin by searching out exhibits in local museums or other collections that have some relevance to that subject.

THE RESOURCES OF A MUSEUM FOR THE STUDENT OF CULTURE

Because contemporary museum exhibits often tell a story or arrange objects according to a few underlying principles, you should familiarize yourself with the organization of the exhibits you view. Different principles underlie the exhibition of objects in different kinds of museums. A fine arts museum, a private collection, a natural history or science museum, an ethnographic museum, a local history or ethnic museum, a university museum, a children's museum—all of them select and arrange their objects differently. In addition, special exhibits are also arranged to tell a particular story. The meaning of an object in the culture that created it may be different from the meaning of that same object in a museum display, and you should be alert to this possibility when you think about items relative to an ethnographic research project.

Very often the beginning of an exhibit will include a written introduction on a wall or in a brochure. In ethnographic and historical museums (and increasingly in art museums as well), wall panels often contain a map and/or a history of the culture that is the subject of the exhibit; they also usually explain the theme(s) of the exhibit and the relations of the objects to the main theme and to each other. Exhibition themes generally focus on important cultural beliefs and practices, so in one sense a lot of the ethnographic work in contemporary museums is done for you.

Where museum exhibits are organized to tell a story or reflect on an ethnographic theme, they may suggest approaches in your ethnographic research that you have not thought about before. Using a museum for ethnographic research is an interactive process: visiting a museum with some ethnographic focus and questions helps shape a visit more constructively, but the very process of looking at and thinking about objects and exhibits in a museum generates new questions and perspectives on an ethnographic research project.

In conjunction with their exhibits, many museums have ongoing videotapes that put the exhibited objects in a more detailed cultural context. For example, the Museum of African Art in New York recently exhibited the ritual art of the Luba of the Congo; a videotape of the ceremonies in which the objects are used accompanied the display. The video was not only ethnographically informative; it also made an immediate impact that would have taken hundreds of pages of print to duplicate. Many museum exhibits also include CD-ROMs, which are accessible from computers in the exhibit itself and which can play the same role as the videotape in the above example.

In large ethnographic or natural-history museums, a geographically related group of cultures may be represented in one room. The South American Room at the American Museum of Natural History in New York, for example, contains culturally accurate and detailed dioramas, including life-sized human figures using displayed objects so that an object's function is immediately understandable. This exhibit room, which includes a continuous video on various aspects of Amazonian culture, is organized around the main aspects of the lives of the peoples of the Amazon region, and the display cases are conveniently divided into the familiar anthropological textbook categories (economics, rituals, social structure, life-cycle ceremonies, and so forth) as they are found among South American horticultural people. It is truly a textbook come alive. In such an exhibit you may gain information relevant to your research project, even if the exact society you are interested in is not represented in its full dimensions.

Even when a museum exhibit is not organized in terms of your own ethnographic interests, the exhibit can still be mined for ethnographic information. The Barry Goldwater Collection of Hopi kachina dolls at the Heard Museum in Phoenix, for example, reflects one individual's tastes with no real ethnographic organization. Nevertheless, the wide range of the collection and the high aesthetic quality of the dolls make them ethnographically significant. You can make your own detailed observations of individual pieces in such an exhibition and follow them up in museum (and other) publications.

Because museum exhibits by their nature are selective, and therefore always limited in their themes, learning from museum exhibits is an active, not a passive experience. In addition to grasping the theme of museum exhibits, you must therefore also interrogate them, asking questions generated by your own interests and from your own point of view. Doing so is particularly necessary in art museums. While ethnographic, local history, or ethnic museums are the most obviously relevant for ethnographic research, art museums also have a great deal to offer an ethnographic project. Indeed, the lines between ethnographic and art museums is blurring with increasing frequency. The material cultures of Africa and Native America, for example, are frequently found in both ethnographic and art museums. Although the latter tend to exhibit objects with much less cultural context than the former and offer less cultural information on their labels, you can still mine these exhibits for ethnographic data by asking anthropological questions about them. For example, the masterpieces of African sculpture in the African Room at the Metropolitan Museum of Art in New York provide ethnographic data in the details of dress, adornment, body decoration, and hairstyles as shown on the figures. They also suggest the significant cultural theme of fertility by the frequent mother/child and male/female groupings.

Descriptive labels—even the minimalist ones found in art museums—are an essential source of ethnographic information. Labels usually give the approximate date of an object, the society in which it was made, the material it is made of, and sometimes a description of how it is used. Labels in ethnographic museums tend to give more information about cultural context, but even in such exhibits you can ask additional questions relevant to your own research interests: Who made the object? For whom was it made? How much was the artist paid for producing it? How was he/she paid? How does the object function in the culture's gender system? Is the object still being used? If it is still used, is it found in the same form or has it been modified in some way? If it is no longer in use, what, if anything, has replaced it? What does the object suggest about the prestige or wealth system of the culture? How were the skills needed to make the object passed on? Was the object used in other than economic exchanges? Was it borrowed? Who could have used it? Was its use restricted in some way, or was it accessible to all? What external influences, if any, are discernible in the object? Is it similar in style to an object in another culture? By seeking answers to such questions, we can move beyond the object to the larger cultural context. You might even be inspired to focus your research on material culture. One advantage to doing so is that people are very often more willing and able to discuss material culture than to talk about social relationships, which may be conflicted, or about ideological issues, which may be too abstract to be easily put into words.

As cultural anthropology and ethnography have developed new concepts, so have ethnographic and art museums. Compared to the simple chronological and technological emphases of earlier exhibits, contemporary museums, like contemporary anthropology, represent culture in complex and dynamic ways. They may highlight, for example, the multifaceted interactions among society, culture, and environments and include cultural variations within geographical regions. These trends are illustrated in a recent exhibit at the Jewish Museum of New York featuring costumes from Morocco. The exhibit theme was the ethnic interrelationships between Jews and Muslims in Morocco as manifested in similarities of dress and adornment. By its very nature, a costume exhibit tells us a great deal about gender roles, prestige and power, and cultural values, but the ethnic interaction theme also included important information on occupational specialization. Because Muslims were forbidden to handle certain kinds of materials, many Jews in Morocco became tailors, and the two communities thus became economically interdependent. This abstract theme is one that would have been difficult to grasp apart from the specific, visible evidence of costumes and jewelry.

This same exhibit illustrates how historical and ethnic museums are becoming more sophisticated. In an earlier era, the historical narratives of museum exhibits mainly represented and legitimated the dominant and elite culture of the nation-state. Museums today are moving toward much more inclusive histories, resulting in increasing space being given to ethnic cultures in large museums and in the creation of museums in the United States focused on ethnic groups in general or on specific ethnic groups that form a substantial part of a local population. For example, the American Museum of Natural History recently featured an exhibit on the voodun ("voodoo") religion, which is practiced in Haiti and other parts of the Caribbean and also among some Caribbean immigrants in the New York City region. In addition to displaying aesthetically exciting objects unfamiliar to most Americans, the museum provided an excellent ethnographic text in the form of extended labels for each item and in the introduction to the exhibit as a whole. The very act of viewing voodun material culture in such a prestigious institution also helped overcome negative stereotypes that many Americans might have held about these religious practices.

These innovative exhibits provide us with new ways of looking at both familiar and unfamiliar items of material culture as we carry out ethnographic fieldwork. The comparative, historical, or other cultural perspectives represented in museum exhibits can put your own ethnographic project into clearer focus in relation to other cultures or to the past.

MUSEUMS AND CULTURE

Human beings transform the world around them to create objects through which they adapt to their environments. As cultural animals, humans also assign meaning and value to the objects they create. The universal human capacity to imagine ideal types—how things *should* be—means that in addition to considerations of practical function, objects are also produced with imagination and skill, and with aesthetic standards in mind. In creating this material culture, humans not only make things, but attempt to make them *well*.

Museums are the repositories of material culture: they were created to collect, preserve, and publicly interpret the wide range of artifacts that represent the best of the past and the present in human societies. The high aesthetic standards that underlie museum collections and exhibits mean that museums provide thrilling encounters with the richness of human culture through its material expression.

The grand and culturally meaningful structures in which many museum collections are displayed themselves add to the special learning environment that museums afford. In Staten Island (in New York City), for example, the permanent collection of the Jacques Marchais Center of Tibetan Art is housed in a building that closely resembles a Tibetan Buddhist mountain temple. The terraced gardens, lily ponds, and view of Lower New York Bay add to the reflective mood required for viewing and appreciating Asian art.

In addition to the intrinsic aesthetic rewards of museums, we should note the innovative organization of contemporary museum exhibitions, the meticulous scholarship that underlies and explains the exhibits, and the presentation of objects that are rare treasures. All these factors mean that museums have become a truly essential source of ethnographic understanding, both of our own and of other cultures.

In addition to the inspiration provided by museums for reflection on the richness of human culture in all its diversity, museums provide an environment for learning largely free of the distractions of modern life. Museums and museum exhibits generally encourage one to linger and to look at an individual pace, allowing for emotional response and reflection that are very different from the sound bites, voice-overs, Muzak, and canned laughter that structure our mental and emotional world. At the same time that the museum can be an individual experience, however, it also lends itself to exploration with family, friends, and classmates, providing an interactive intellectual experience.

THE POLITICS OF CULTURE: MUSEUMS AND THE REPRESENTATION OF CULTURE

There is now a general consensus in anthropology that the representation of cultures is a kind of political act: it emerges from particular positions of power and it has political effects. The politics of culture can be seen in the ways in which museums choose to represent cultures in and of themselves and in relation to one another. The cultural representations offered by art, ethnographic, and historical museums are now frequently subjects of controversy, the dimensions of which reveal new thinking about the roles of museums in American society and conflicts over important cultural values. Museum collections, and particularly museum exhibits, are now critically examined for what they say about the cultures they aim to represent. As conflicts over culture and power continue, museums and museum exhibits themselves are becoming interesting subjects for ethnographic research.

Museums, like other cultural institutions, have particular histories. They originated as national treasure houses, scientific institutions, cabinets of curiosities, preservers of "disappearing" cultures, and individual or family collections. Museums also operate within many cultural contexts, including fluctuating art markets, politically charged funding policies, competition with commercial ventures such as theme parks, and, to some extent, the theories of social scientists. All of these contexts influence museum collections, conservation practices, financing policies, scholarly research, hiring practices, and, most important of all, the exhibitions themselves. All of these contexts are worth examining ethnographically.

The early organization of ethnographic displays in natural history and ethnography museums, for example, tended to be evolutionary, suggesting a hierarchy of cultures. This approach has given way under a barrage of criticism to other, more complex organizing principles, such as those noted above in the Jewish Museum and the voodun exhibits. The representation of indigenous peoples, for example, was mainly in terms of master narratives of cultural disappearance, an approach now giving way to empowering stories of revival, remembrance, and struggle. Museums have been created by the indigenous people themselves; other museums (such as the Ellis Island Museum in New York's harbor) have been created to celebrate the very concept of ethnic diversity. Such museums are based on the idea that victims of genocide, oppression, and colonialism can use museums as important sources of revitalized cultural identities and to tell their stories to a wider public.

Because museums are such important and influential culture brokers, controversy rages over whether they are the only proper arbiters of how a culture should be exhibited. In spite of some protests by curators, consultation and collaboration with cultural communities represented in museum exhibits is now an accepted practice in ethnographic (and some art) museums. The interaction between museums and the people they represent has become particularly charged with the passage of the Native American Graves Protection and Repatriation Act (NAGPRA), a law that requires the return of human remains and other cultural objects to the groups from which they were taken.

New anthropological approaches to the study of material culture include consideration of the following questions: How do items identified as "ceremonial objects" become part of the symbolic process through which nation-states establish hegemony (i.e., an image of the approved "mainstream" way to do things)? How do material objects function as emblems of social class and ethnic or national identity? How have European and North American ethnographic and art museum exhibits manifested colonial views of non-Western peoples, particularly through the notion of "the primitive"?

One of the most controversial exhibits was "Primitivism in Twentieth Century Art: Affinities of the Tribal and the Modern" featured at New York's Museum of Modern Art in 1984. The exhibit curators claimed that it was a tribute to the "primitive" to put "tribal" art in a prestigious art museum context and show how it influenced some of the West's greatest contemporary artists. Nevertheless, critics pointed out that the repression of the context, meaning, content, function, and individual authorship of tribal art, and the emphasis on aesthetic style distorted tribal cultures. For example, the absence of cultural context reinforces the separation between art and other aspects of culture, which may be characteristic in Western culture, but certainly not in tribal cultures. The Western museum's preoccupation with the antique, the pure, and the authentic in tribal art also grows out of a Western capitalist system of values that ignores the values and voices of those it claims to celebrate by displaying their art.

These criticisms are widely expressed by Native Americans in the United States. They claim that typical art museum exhibits of Native American art represent their societies as timeless, rather than changing. They further point out that such exhibits do not include Native American voices in either consultative or collaborative roles, that they neglect contemporary artists, that they display objects collected under questionable circumstances, that they display sacred/religious objects that should not be seen by the public, and that they ignore any representation of contemporary political issues. Unlike these typical art museums, the National Museum of the American Indian built its permanent collection, "All Roads are Good," around objects selected by Native Americans, and the labels highlight the responses of the latter to those objects. In a similar fashion, Native American museums, such as the Cherokee Museum in Cherokee, North Carolina, emphasize the dynamics of Native American history, particularly the changing ecological and historical dimensions of Native American cultures in the period of European contact, an approach almost entirely absent in art museum exhibits of Native American material culture.

An outstanding example of what can be achieved in museum exhibits that include collaboration with indigenous communities was the 1991 American Museum of Natural History exhibit, "The Enduring Potlatch," which included not only masterworks of Northwest Coast art and scholarly information pertinent to an understanding of that art, but also presented dioramas of contemporary potlatches replete with plastic utensils and mass-produced blankets. The display also included a properly contextualized exhibit of the Canadian government's repression of the potlatch and the confiscation of potlatch items, which have subsequently been returned to Northwest Coast groups. None of this additional historical context in any way detracted from the artistic quality of the exhibition, which was superb, and it added a much more accurate historical picture. The potlatch exhibit, and others like it (e.g., "Aztec: The World of Moctezuma" at the Denver Museum of Natural History in 1991–92 at the height of the Columbus quincentenary controversy over the contact between Europeans and Native Americans, and the historical representations thereof), indicate that museums can hold to their traditional mandates of collecting and displaying the best of human artistic creations and at the same time present historically and ethnographically accurate representations of cultures. These new perspectives on museums as themselves representing the cultures of which they are a part makes the study of museums and their exhibits important subjects for ethnographic research, and I acknowledge with thanks Stanley Freed, Glen Peterson, Beth Pacheco, and Paisley Gregg for sharing their ideas on museums with me as I prepared this chapter.

YOUR PROJECT

Your assignment is to complete the following two-step exercise.

1. Visit any ethnographic, historical, natural science, art, or ethnic museum in your locality. Select any one object (or group of related objects) on exhibit that is of interest to you. Write a detailed description of its appearance, form, composition, style, function, and cultural context (including the meanings and values attached to it). Conclude

with a list of questions you would like to ask someone from the culture that produced that object.

2. Write a brief prospectus for organizing an ethnographic exhibit devoted to your own culture. What would be the theme of your exhibit? What objects would you use in the exhibit to carry that theme through and why would you choose these objects in particular (keeping in mind both aesthetic and culturally relevant criteria)? What kind of space would you design for your project? What media would you choose to accompany the exhibit (e.g., video, seminars, children's educational programs, photographs)? Whom might you ask to collaborate or consult on this project?

A FEW SELECTED READINGS FOR FURTHER INFORMATION

Center for Arts and Culture. 2000. *The Politics of Culture: Policy Perspectives for Individuals, Institutions, and Communities*. Washington, DC: New Press.

Clifford, James. 1997. *Routes*. Cambridge, MA: Harvard University Press.

Day, Jane Stevenson. 1994. Interpreting Culture: New Voices in Museums. *Journal of Arts, Management, Law and Society* 23(4):307–316.

Dubin, Steven C. 1999. *Displays of Power: Memory and Amnesia in the American Museum*. New York: New York University Press.

Jones, Anna Laura. 1993. Exploding Canons: The Anthropology of Museums. *Annual Review of Anthropology* 22:201–220.

Marcus, George E., and Fred R. Myers, eds. 1995. *The Traffic in Culture: Refiguring Art and Anthropology*. Berkeley: University of California Press.

Price, Sally. 1989. *Primitive Art in Civilized Places*. Chicago: University of Chicago Press.

Stocking, George W., ed. 1985. *Objects and Others: Essays on Museums and Material Culture*. Madison: University of Wisconsin Press.

7

Learning about Formal Organizations

V. Richard Persico, Jr.

A RESEARCH PROJECT

I have had a longstanding interest in the regional culture of the American South. One of the cultural traits that has traditionally characterized the region is its emphasis on race as the principal determinant of social status. Other status indicators such as gender, occupation, wealth, or education have been secondary to race. Racial stratification has permeated all aspects of life in the South, including work, recreation, religion, and politics. In the years since the civil rights movement of the 1960s, however, this pattern has been changing for various reasons, and this change has been a principal concern of my research. I had just finished a project focusing on race, stratification, and occupation in a rural Southern community and was taking a little vacation when I met an old friend whom I had not seen in several years. He was working in an urban Southern hospital. After spending some time with him and learning a bit about his work environment, I decided that his hospital would be a good place in which to study race, stratification, and occupation in an urban setting. The primary object of my research was not the formal organization of the hospital itself. The hospital was, rather, the arena in which social and cultural processes took place. Nevertheless, that arena affected the processes, and its characteristics had to be taken into account.

General Hospital is a mid-sized, general-purpose community hospital located in a medium-sized Southern city. It is equipped with a full range of laboratories (e.g., radiology, magnetic imaging). The local emergency medical service is based there and it is equipped with a full-service emergency room. It is, in every way, a modern hospital. The community it serves is typical of many Southern cities of its size. It maintains a keen sense of history and tradition while grappling with the economic, political, and other social issues of a rapidly changing region. Issues of race are among the most important that face the community. The assignment of roles in the community has traditionally been based on the caste-like relationships that existed between black and white populations, but this pattern is now challenged by law and by new economic realities. The changes, however, have been so rapid and so great in scope that many people are uncertain about how status is now to be allocated; they are confused about how to act toward categories of people defined by new and uncertain criteria. The staff of General Hospital reflected these uncertainties in their assignment of statuses and roles within the hospital's social structure.

When I studied the history of the hospital, I learned that race had never been an explicit criterion of status allocation within its formal organizational structure. In the days of legal segregation, it was unnecessary to specify in writing which positions were reserved for persons of which race. With the end of legal segregation, formal racial criteria for status allocation became illegal in public institutions such as General Hospital. Officially, the hospital was an equal-opportunity, affirmative-action employer. Its organization and activities were based entirely on rational, bureaucratic criteria. Nevertheless, *de facto* segregation, which always had been the rule in the informal structure, remained strong long after the end of *de jure* segregation. "White-collar and white-uniform" positions (i.e., administrative, clerical, and professional medical positions) were traditionally reserved for white people. "Blue-collar and colored-uniform" positions were for blacks. Members of other non-white ethnic groups were so rare in this community as to be insignificant. By the time of my research, however, around twenty years after the end of legal segregation, things were changing rapidly. The community had become larger and more diverse. A generation that had grown up without the practice of legal segregation was entering the workforce. Race was still a criterion of status allocation, but it was no longer the master criterion it once had been.

Stratification within the informal organizational structure was the main focus of my research. At the outset, I expected to find that race was still the primary *de facto* criterion for status allocation within the informal system, with gender being the next in importance. I expected that formal occupational status would generally conform to racial stratification. The higher status white-collar positions would be occupied by whites, and the lower blue-collar positions by blacks. I anticipated that there would be occupational stratification within the racial stratification. But where whites held blue-collar jobs, I expected that they would rank above blacks in similar positions. During the course of my research, however, I discovered that while race remained a significant variable in the organization's informal stratification system, it was being displaced as a master criterion by other factors, leading to some confusion about relative status.

To study the informal dimension of this formal organization, I took a job at General Hospital. As my major interest was the status hierarchy among the blue-collar staff, I became a "wash man," a person who ran the large-capacity industrial washing machines in the hospital laundry. The Laundry Department also had "press women" who ironed and folded the sheets, towels, gowns, and surgical drapes (cloths used to cover patients during surgery or while giving birth). The other main groups of blue-collar workers were in the Housekeeping Department (maids and janitors), the Maintenance Department, the Food Service Department, and the Grounds Department. The administrators, secretaries, and dietitians in these departments were, of course, white-collar workers and were not the focus of my study.

To outward appearances, the hospital appeared to be stratified according to the same sort of combined caste-class system typical of the traditional South. The most important criterion of stratification in this system was color, with whites constituting the upper caste and having access to more wealth, prestige, and power than blacks, who make up the lower caste. Each caste is cross-cut by class divisions. Upper-class whites and upper-class blacks, for example, share essentially the same socioeconomic characteristics, although the black upper class is much smaller than that of the whites, and the black lower class is larger than that of the whites. The caste line, however, places the black classes at a disadvantage with respect to comparable white classes. Not only do blacks have to defer to whites of the same class, but in many social contexts, a black person of the upper class must defer to a white person of the lower class. In this system, race is the master status. At General Hospital, almost all of the blue-collar workers were black, and almost all of the white-collar workers were white. The only exception appeared to be the Maintenance Department which, while blue-collar, was all white. They were, however, better paid than any of the other blue-collar workers. It therefore appeared that the caste line was intact, with whites dominating the more desirable and better-paying jobs, and blacks being relegated to the less desirable, lower-paying positions.

My first indication that another criterion was being used for master status allocation came during the orientation session. New employees, from doctors to maids, were required to participate in this program, and everyone attended the same session at which administrators reviewed policy and procedure, employees filled out forms, and everyone took a CPR course. I sat next to a man who was joining the staff as an Emergency Room physician. He was friendly, and we worked together on the CPR course. When I next saw him, he was wearing his white M.D. coat and I was wearing my blue wash-man outfit. Not only did he not speak—he would not even make eye contact with me. At first, I took his behavior to be snobbishness on his part, but I subsequently observed that no physician, regardless of race, would speak to or even notice a blue-collar worker, including the white maintenance staff. Nurses and technicians also followed this pattern. Nurses would give brief instructions to maids and janitors when necessary, but exchanges of pleasantries were very rare. The race of the medical-staff person and the race of the blue-collar worker seemed to matter not at all. What mattered was the color of the uniform. People who wore white did not interact with those who wore colors.

My next indication that another criterion for master status was being used came when I worked my first Saturday shift. The press women worked so fast that they could press in one shift as much as the wash men could wash in two shifts. There was only one wash man per shift. A wash man worked a single shift alone on Saturday to stay ahead of the pressers, who had the weekend off. I had been shown the dirty linen rooms on all the floors, but I forgot where half of them were. I was getting behind in collecting laundry when several janitors began bringing dirty laundry to me. They welcomed me to the job and told me to call on them if I needed help. Later that day, a maid dropped by to use my laundry scale to weigh herself and she offered to get me some ice cream. I accepted her offer, but before I could get my money out, she was gone. She came back in a few minutes with three cups of ice cream, one chocolate, one strawberry, and one vanilla. When I offered to pay her, she told me not to be silly. She had gotten the ice cream from the third floor nursing station. Stealing ice cream from the nursing stations was a favorite sport of the housekeeping staff. They shared their booty with the other wearers of colored uniforms. Later, in the employees' cafeteria, the line server gave me a portion of roast beef that was twice the size of one given to the E.R. technician who was just in front of me in line. People who wore colored uniforms got better service from the line servers than people who wore white. The most important criterion for deciding who was on which side in the contest of "us" versus "them" was not the color of a person's skin, but the color of his or her uniform. Occupation seemed to be replacing race as the chief criterion for stratification, although race was still clearly a factor. The blue-collar workers who were black regarded me as a bit of an oddity because I was white, but not on the maintenance crew. Nevertheless, despite my oddity, I was still more to be trusted than any white-collar person. I could be given booty looted from the preserves of the white collars. I could be recruited to help in the contest.

My place in the blue-collar stratum was assured when the emergency medical technicians who worked on the ambulance complained that I was not putting enough starch in their white uniforms. Only a fool would challenge a real hospital wash man to use more starch. The press women reported my response to the rest of the blue-collar world. The next load of uniforms I washed could stand alone after they were pressed. Indeed, they were substantially harder than boards. All the blue-collar workers, including the maintenance staff, congratulated me on having done the right thing. Indeed, I got much better service from all of them after this incident. I also washed their uniforms. The EMS staff thanked me for my prompt attention to their request, but asked that I return to my old, inadequate levels of starch.

At General Hospital, race was no longer the most important thing about a person. It was still a criterion for status allocation, but it was receding in importance to the level of such variables as gender or education. Occupation was becoming the master status criterion. Even a white, college-educated anthropologist could be denigrated as a lowly wash man by the medical elites, and that same white wash man could achieve a measure of respect and even admiration among the largely black blue-collar workers by playing by the blue-collar rules. The crosscutting of the traditional race, class, and ethnic strata by occupational strata produced considerable confusion and discomfort in role behavior and status assignment. This confusion did not produce a more egalitarian system, but rather a more complex one with less consensus about the criteria for status allocation.

STUDYING FORMAL ORGANIZATIONS: A BRIEF HISTORY

Anthropologists have traditionally focused their research on small-scale societies or on the grassroots level of larger societies. In such settings, social interaction is usually carried out in small, informal primary groups such as families or neighborhoods. Formal organizations, such as corporations and bureaucracies, have more typically been the research focus of sociologists. Nevertheless, whenever anthropologists have studied larger, more complex societies, they have carried out research in formal organizations, not only to understand how those organizations themselves work, but also to explore larger social and cultural processes that might be played out in microcosm in the organizations. There have been, among many other examples, anthropological studies of bureaucratic organizations in African polities; the European space program; educational institutions; and business corporations. The study of formal organizations is a good approach for researching a number of phenomena in complex social and cultural systems. Formal organizations comprise a large proportion of their social structure and perform a variety of critical tasks. Much of the social interaction within these complex systems takes place within the context of formal organizations.

Formal organizations are groups designed to achieve particular goals. They are a dominant aspect of urban, industrial societies, but may be found in other types of societies as well. A social group, as opposed to a simple aggregation of people, has a number of distinguishing characteristics. Its members interact on a regular basis over a period of time, share a sense of collective identity, and share a number of rights by virtue of common membership. Perhaps most important, the group has a degree of internal organizational structure. In a formal organization, this structure has officially designated positions and formal rules designed to coordinate the activities of the members in achieving the organization's goals. Informal groups tend to be small, with interaction based on primary, personal, face-to-face relationships. Formal organizations are typically large and impersonal, with most interaction carried out via secondary relationships. Because they are designed to achieve well defined goals, their social structure tends to be rational and bureaucratic. They can, however, vary widely in their size, objectives, and degree of bureaucratization.

Classic sociological theory identified the following characteristics as typical of bureaucracies. There is a clear-cut division of labor such that each member of the organization has a specialized job and concentrates on his/her specific task. There is a hierarchy of authority, with the few individuals at the top having much greater authority than the larger number at the bottom. The scope of an individual's authority is clearly defined such that each member receives orders from the official immediately above and is responsible for those members immediately below. An elaborate system of formal, written rules and regulations governs day-to-day functioning, and all decisions are based on these rules and on established precedents for interpreting the rules. The members of the organization remain impersonal in their contacts with the public, treating clients as "cases" rather than as individuals. Members of the organization adopt a detached attitude toward one another, interacting more on the basis of their roles within the organization than as individuals and excluding personal feelings from official decision-making processes. Exhaustive written records, preferably in standardized format, are kept of all activities pertaining to the organization. There is a specialized administrative staff of managers, secretaries, and others whose sole function is to keep the organization running smoothly. Employees are accustomed to anticipate a career within the organization. Candidates for positions in the hierarchy are selected on the basis of seniority and/or merit rather than favoritism, family connections, or other personal criteria.

The anthropological study of formal organizations typically focuses on the arrangement of social statuses and the performance of their associated roles within the organization. A status is a position within a social system. Every individual occupies a number of such positions simultaneously and a series of them throughout the course of life. Each status is associated with a corresponding role, a set of expected behaviors appropriate to the occupant of the status. In a formal organization, statuses and roles are ideally a function of the organization's rational plan for carrying out the activities for which it is constituted. In practice, however, this ideal arrangement is typically accompanied by a parallel informal structure that will have additional, and sometimes competing, objectives. This parallel structure is often based on the informal, primary relationships that inevitably develop between individuals within the organizational structure. This informal structure often has as much impact on the operation of the organization as its formal structure—and sometimes more. A famous study of the Hawthorne plant of Western Electric Company was carried out between 1927 and 1932; it was an early demonstration of the importance of the informal structure. The workers who wired telephone switchboards, for example, had their output determined not by the rules of the company but by informal norms that had developed among them. Workers who worked too fast were called "rate busters," while those who worked too slow were considered "chiselers." These names were accompanied by informal sanctions that defined the rights and duties of members of the work crew as effectively as any of the company's official rules.

More recent research confirms the importance of the informal structure in a formal organization. As members come to know one another as individuals, they alter or circumvent the formal structure and its rules to suit individual needs and wishes. Workers develop their own definition of such matters as how long a "lunch hour" should last, and how much or what kinds of company property can be appropriated for personal use. They use their personal networks to get around the chain of command, gain extra privileges, or enhance their prestige. The informal structure may actually increase the efficiency of the organization by cutting red tape and improving worker morale by humanizing an otherwise cold and uncomfortable work environment. On the other hand, it may divert resources and energy into activities that lie outside of or even work counter to the stated objectives of the organization. In carrying out research on a formal organization, it is necessary to understand both the formal and informal social structures and how they relate to one another.

STUDYING FORMAL ORGANIZATIONS: THE PROCESS

Conducting research in a formal organization requires gaining an understanding of both its ideal and its actual systems. Because a formal organization is a social group explicitly constituted to achieve particular goals, its ideal objectives and structure are relatively easy to determine. Discovering its informal goals and its actual, functioning arrangement of statuses and roles is more challenging because these factors are typically unwritten, unstated, and not systematically understood, even by participants. Organization members often deny, at least for the record, that any such informal dimension exists. They may consider investigation into this aspect of their organization to be a threat to them individually or to the organization as a whole. It is therefore very important for the researcher to develop a plan of research that avoids causing harm or embarrassment to individuals involved in the study.

The first step in studying a formal organization is to determine its ideal objectives. In many organizations, there is a formal charter or mission statement that is published and easily available to the public. At General Hospital, the mission statement was couched in very lofty terms and published in a number of formats. Such language is typical of mission statements, which are then operationalized through a set of goals that constitute an action plan. General Hospital set forth its mission statement in three parts: vision, mission, and values. "Vision" was stated very concisely: "General Hospital will be the leader in health care delivery, committed to excellence and dedicated to continuously improving the health, wellness and quality of life of our community."

"Mission" elaborated on that statement and specified what was to be done to achieve the vision:

> While striving to be an outstanding health care system, the mission of General Hospital is to provide to its patients, their sponsors, its medical staff and the community quality patient care and a scope of services that are of a superior value, delivered in a caring and safe atmosphere with dignity and compassion by competent professionals. The credibility and reputation of General Hospital are of the utmost importance to those served by the institution and its supporters. Based on the continuous assessment of community needs by management, the medical staff, and the governing body, General Hospital shall diversify and provide selected health care programs within the defined region. General Hospital strives for excellence, patient satisfaction and a sound financial position.

The statement of "values" spelled out the qualities that would make it possible to carry out this mission (e.g., excellence, honesty and integrity, continuous improvement, efficiency and effectiveness, teamwork) and explained what activities would be entailed in living out those values (e.g., creating a safe environment where care and service are delivered with respect and dignity; communicating openly and honestly; embracing change as an opportunity for improvement; striving for accuracy; encouraging personal and professional development). In sum, "understanding and demonstrating these values is the shared responsibility of all employees and persons affiliated with General Hospital. This institution will recognize and reward individuals whose exceptional performance clearly reflects their ongoing commitment to these values." The aims were to be facilitated by a set of written rules and regulations setting forth standard operating procedures for each department of the hospital. Some of these rules were provided to employees in a handbook, and others were in a procedure manuals kept in various departmental offices as well as in the central administrative office.

The second step in studying a formal organization is to determine its ideal structure for meeting its objectives, which is typically set out in the form of a table of organization that defines the hierarchy of authority. Each position within the organization (its various "statuses") has a job description (its expected behaviors) attached to it. Like the mission statement, the table of organization and the descriptions of the various rights and duties of each position are usually available in such formats as employee handbooks or shareholder reports. Since General Hospital is publicly owned, these data were easily accessible. On its organizational chart, each employee position, from director to janitor, has a job description, including minimum qualifications, specific responsibilities, and the range of compensation. These descriptions, along with the written standard operating procedures, represent the ideal role behaviors expected from each member of the organization.

Anyone working in or with a formal organization soon discovers that it seldom operates entirely according to its ideal structure and standardized procedures. People deal with one another both as individuals and as occupants of particular statuses within an organization. They seek shortcuts around cumbersome procedures. For example, it may be common knowledge among members of the organization that someone in a position of authority is difficult to approach, inflexible, or perhaps even incompetent. That person may be indirectly approached through a trusted assistant or secretary, or may be circumvented altogether. A common saying at General Hospital was, "It's easier to get forgiveness than permission." This attitude did not, however, suggest that anything that worked was all right. Formal organizations always have ways both explicit and tacit for dealing with those whose rule bending becomes intolerable. In any event, it is important to realize that there is an informal, implicit structure and set of procedures that parallels the formal set. The description of that informal dimension reveals as much—or more—about the organization and the cultural phenomena under investigation than a description of the formal, stated arrangements. A variety of data-collection techniques such as those treated elsewhere in this book can be used to gather data on the informal dimension of a formal organization.

YOUR PROJECT

Choose a formal organization with a readily accessible mission statement and table of organization. Many public organizations such as government agencies, schools (including your own university), and hospitals publish these documents. Documents from private organizations such as law offices, newspapers, department stores, or distribution centers may be less easily obtained, although it is certainly not impossible to do so. In all cases, approach the person in charge of dealing with the public, explain your project, and ask for the information. In most cases, you will have no problem getting the data. If you are refused, thank your contact person and go elsewhere. Write up a report in which you discuss what you can learn about the culture of this organization from its formal, published documents. Then discuss in detail how you would go about conducting an in-depth study of the informal dimension of the operation of this organization. Reflect on the various data-collection strategies you might use. Be sure to include a consideration of any ethical problems that might be involved in sharing this information with members of the organization, and propose ways to resolve such conflicts.

A FEW SELECTED READINGS FOR FURTHER INFORMATION

Bruun, Ole. 1993. *Business and Bureaucracy in a Chinese City: An Ethnography of Private Business Households in Contemporary China.* Berkeley: University of California Institute of East Asian Studies.

Chang, Heewon. 1992. *Adolescent Life and Ethos: An Ethnography of a U.S. High School.* Philadelphia: Falmer.

Fallers, Lloyd A. 1965. *Bantu Bureaucracy: A Century of Political Evolution among the Basoga of Uganda.* Chicago: University of Chicago Press.

———. 1974. *The Social Anthropology of the Nation-State.* Chicago: Aldine.

Lien, Marianne. 1997. *Marketing and Modernity: An Ethnography of Marketing Practice.* Oxford: Berg.

Roethlisberger, Fritz J., and William J. Dickson. 1939. *Management and the Worker.* Cambridge: Harvard University Press.

Schwartzman, Helen B. 1993. *Ethnography in Organizations.* Newbury Park, CA: Sage.

Scott, W. Richard, and Søren Christensen, eds. 1995. *The Institutional Construction of Organizations: International and Longitudinal Studies.* Thousand Oaks, CA: Sage.

Trice, Harrison Miller, and Janice M. Beyer. 1993. *The Cultures of Work Organizations.* Englewood Cliffs, NJ: Prentice-Hall.

Weber, Max. 1978. *Economy and Society: An Outline of Interpretive Sociology,* ed. Guenther Roth and Claus Wittich, trans. Ephraim Fischoff. Berkeley: University of California Press.

Zabusky, Stacia E. 1995. *Launching Europe: An Ethnography of European Cooperation in Space Science.* Princeton, NJ: Princeton University Press.

8

Free-Listing Vocabulary

J. Jerome Smith

A RESEARCH PROJECT

A long time ago in a place far, far away, a young anthropology student began a year of doctoral dissertation research on inheritance practices. The place was Rota, an island in the Marianas chain in the region of the Pacific known as Micronesia. I was the student—and nobody died. While I could not be unhappy at the health and vitality of the island's 1100 inhabitants, I was understandably concerned that a cultural account of intergenerational property transactions might not be forthcoming. If the very customs I wanted to describe did not happen to occur while I was there, what recourse did I have? I soon found myself engaged in that most fundamental human activity—talk.

Of course it really is not surprising that the Rotanese and I should talk about inheritance. Even if I had been able to observe numerous instances of actual inheritance transactions, I would have found it necessary to talk about what I was observing to more fully understand the process and the people who were engaged in it. In fact, one of the defining qualities of the human condition is that most of what we come to know and share about the world— our culture, in other words—emerges out of talk with others. When doing ethnography, therefore, it is important to keep in mind that while people's statements about the nature of their world may not be *all* the data, they certainly represent excellent samplings of that larger whole.

This early lesson in ethnographic research led me to become increasingly interested in language and in the role of the lexicon as a structured repository of cultural knowledge. To this end I have more recently become involved in exploring cultural domains, which are large categories of objects, activities, or feelings that people use to organize the cultural knowledge that they share with one another. They are extremely important in gaining an understanding of a culture, because they are the resources people use to access and activate their cultural knowledge. Moreover, they are readily accessible to the ethnographer by way of vocabulary.

A direct and useful way of building up the structure and content of cultural domains such as kinship, transportation, pronouns, animals, foods, or colors is by means of free-listing. This technique allows for the systematic gathering of verbal data by asking people to "list all the kinds of X you know about," where X is a cultural domain that you have reason to believe is relevant to the members of the community you are studying. Keep in mind that "reason to believe" is often no more than an educated guess; like all things cultural, it is difficult to know prior to immersion in the field setting what the domains will be, much less what will be in them and how they will be organized internally. For instance, Americans would generally consider hot dogs and hamburgers as members of a domain of food, and could probably further classify them as distinctive from other foods, such as filet mignon or shrimp scampi. They would generally not be comfortable with a grouping of hot dogs and cocker spaniels into any common cultural domain—and certainly not into one of foods, even though to the outsider both seem to refer to some sort of canine. In order to figure out what cultural domains there are in a particular culture and what their structure and content is like, we need to ask people about them. One of the most straightforward approaches for doing so is simply to ask people what is in a domain that you want to know about; free-listing is a systematic word-collecting method to help you do so. Free-listing is an approach to the definition and exploration of cultural domains based on how people talk about them and their contents. It is a valuable method for establishing empirically how people organize the world they live in. It is only the beginning, however, of an effort to understand how people acquire and share symbolically structured knowledge and use it to work with one another in their daily lives.

FREE-LISTING AS A TOOL OF ETHNOGRAPHIC RESEARCH

For most of the twentieth century, linguists and anthropologists argued that semantic systems (largely expressed through vocabulary) were free to vary from language to language without much constraint from factors like biology, geography, or sociocultural complexity. To know the semantics of a language, one had to go out and study it. Moreover, these unpredictable systems had a limiting—if not determining—effect on how the people who spoke a particular language would view the world and act in it. That is, the worldview of a people was built up relative to the language they spoke.

One example of this kind of relativism that has been studied in great detail over the years is color terminology. The rainbow can be described in a seeming infinity of ways, depending on the color terms provided by a given language. All humans are physically capable of seeing the same colors, but they do not—cannot—describe what they see in the same way, given the diversity of terminologies available to them. For instance, English speakers have words like "blue" and "green" to distinguish the colors of the sky and the grass. When the Navajo, however, designate the color of either the sky or the grass, they generally employ a single color term we might translate as "grue" (greenish blue or bluish green), unless they want to go to the extra trouble of a lengthy comparative phrase further distinguishing the color of the sky from the color of the grass. Any speaker of any language can make such elaborate distinctions, but to do so they may have to go beyond the ordinary vocabulary. For example, I might point to a reddish stain on a wall and say, "That stain looks like the rust on my aunt's old Chevrolet." If you know my aunt and if you have seen her old car, then you will know exactly what I have in mind. But if you have never met her or seen her car, my elaborate simile will be lost on you, and I might just as well say, "reddish," a slightly modified version of a common color term.

Every language has its own way of organizing the spectrum terminologically, using different words and phrases to cover different areas of the rainbow. The semantic systems of different languages—at least with regard to color, although probably with regard to all domains—are therefore free to vary independently of one another. As a result, the members of different cultures "see" the colorful world differently and deal with it in ways peculiar to themselves and to the languages they speak.

In 1969, however, two researchers, Brent Berlin and Paul Kay, published *Basic Color Terms*, a study that turned the idea of linguistic relativity on its ear. Using primary and secondary data from a large number of languages, Berlin and Kay argued that, far from being unconstrained in their diversity, the color terminologies of different languages had some very patterned characteristics in common. They reminded us that there are indeed many ways in which colors can be described and designated—including such esoteric phrases as "the color of the rust on my aunt's old Chevrolet." But it would serve no purpose, they claimed, to continue to worry about these limitless possibilities. Instead, they introduced the notion of basic color terms and asked questions about their occurrence in different languages. For a color term to be considered "basic," it must satisfy the following main criteria: 1) it must be a single word (e.g., in English, "red" but not "bluish green"); 2) it must be at the top of the color taxonomy (e.g., in English, "blue," which cannot refer to any color other than itself, but not "khaki," which is a blended kind of green); 3) it must be abstract and broadly applicable (e.g., in English, "yellow" can describe any kind of object, unlike "blonde," which can typically refer only to hair); 4) it must be salient (e.g., in English, "green" is a term speakers think of early and consistently when they think about colors, but "taupe" is a term that only a few speakers know about and which is used only in very special situations).

The basic color terms in English are said to be red, blue, yellow, green, white, black, brown, purple, pink, orange, and gray. In their review of ninety-eight other languages, Berlin and Kay found that the number of basic terms ranges from two to eleven. The color ranges encoded by basic terms were tied to the number of terms. Thus, some languages had only two basic terms, and they invariably designated the dark ("black") and the light ("white") colors. Three-term systems included black, white, and red. Four-term systems included these three plus either green or yellow. Six-term systems add blue. Seven-term systems add brown. Systems with eight to eleven terms add purple, pink, orange, and gray in one combination or another.

The focal points for these color terms (e.g., the "bluest blue") were very stable across the languages, while the boundaries (where one color begins to be regarded as something else) were more variable. These patterns suggest a biological basis for color terminology rooted in the nature of human color vision and not subject to the whims of cultural and linguistic variation. The partially fixed order of expansion of basic color term categories from two to eleven suggests an equally patterned progression of historical growth within given languages.

The findings of Berlin and Kay stimulated a considerable amount of further research. I was impressed by the originality and thoroughness of their work, although I had some questions about their methods as well as about their conclusions. Given my interest in lexical semantics, I was struck by the way they settled on the set of basic color terms for any particular language. I found their arguments and criteria for the basic terms to be compelling, but I was concerned that they might have taken some of the empirical confirmation of their ideas a little bit for granted.

The first three criteria—one-word long, taxonomically superior, and widely applicable terms—could be tested pretty quickly with knowledgeable informants. The criterion of salience, however, seemed to me to be assumed once the first three were satisfied. Berlin and Kay cited no empirical studies specifically focused on the salience of basic color terms, and I was unaware of any such studies. Nobody seems to have looked directly at the question of just which color terms would show up early and consistently when people were asked to name them. In conjunction with colleagues at the University of Missouri–Columbia, I decided to use a free-listing technique involving English color terms in order to address this question of salience.

FREE-LISTING: THE PROCESS

We gathered English color term free-lists from 353 students in linguistics and anthropology classes at the University of South Florida and the University of Missouri–Columbia. Students were asked to write down as many color terms as they could think of in two minutes; they averaged nineteen color terms in their lists, for a total of 6,822 responses. Using a measure combining the average frequency and order of mention of color terms, we assigned a salience index (Smith's S) to each of the 487 color terms listed by one or more students and ranked the terms accordingly. The results of our study were both confirming and more broadly informative. The twelve most salient terms included the eleven terms proposed by Berlin and Kay as basic English color terms—just as they would argue on the basis of salience. Only the term "violet" intruded into this top echelon of salience terms.

A more unexpected outcome was the degree to which the overall ordering of more salient to less salient color terms was associated with an increase in their structural and semantic complexity. We first eliminated 278 terms mentioned by only one student. The remaining 209 terms were mentioned by two or more students, making them at least minimally culturally salient, given our understanding of culture as shared knowledge. Generally speaking, the simpler the term—both structurally and semantically—the higher its salience ranking. Thus, the basic color terms are structurally simple (one word) and semantically simple (referring only to the abstract category of the color itself). Moving down the salience ranking, one-word terms begin to have more complex meanings, now designating color concretely by way of specific objects (e.g., "gold," "peach," "coral"). Structurally more complex items of two or more words emerge much lower on the salience ordering and often have very elaborate object/color referents (e.g., "candy apple red," "sea foam green," "electric blue"). The broad association of salience with simplicity was quite striking and not something we fully anticipated when we undertook our more restricted examination of basic color terms through free-listing.

YOUR PROJECT

To conduct your own free-listing research you will need a domain to study and a group of people who share cultural knowledge about it and who are willing to spend a little time going through the exercise with you. Before getting started, be sure to consult with your instructor to make sure that all the required informed consent procedures have been followed.

For free-listing data to be useful, you will need to obtain information from twenty to thirty informants. Introductory anthropology courses are probably your best bet for finding such participants, since students are usually eager to see anthropology at work, and you can return later to share your results. Introductory psychology courses, which often integrate research activity into their plans, are another possibility. If you have access to local primary and secondary schools and official permission to work with their students, such sites may be good places to conduct the study, as language data from younger people can be particularly revealing of basic cultural patterns. At the other end of the age spectrum, congregate living facilities for senior citizens can also be excellent sites, as the residents are often eager to find new things to do and are more than willing to share what they know with younger people.

Well-patterned results are most likely to be obtained from a study of domains in the natural and material world. Just as color is a domain of the senses, domains of birds, animals, furniture, or automobiles involve concrete objects that are easily discussed and relatively unambiguous in meaning. Keep your domain scope large and generic. It is better, for example, to explore the domain of dogs than the domain of terriers.

The easiest approach is to present your domain to everyone in a group and then ask for individual written lists of the items to be included. Working with one informant at a time or gathering oral data for later transcription may sometimes be necessary, but these procedures are very time-consuming and labor-intensive, and should be avoided if at all possible. It is important to be as systematic about the exercise as possible, especially if you will be working with more than one group. Your introductory remarks should be as brief as possible—do not give people your own examples of what might go on the list, as they will then probably follow your lead, even if they would not have generated the same items on their own.

You will want to enter the data you receive into some kind of standard format, and you will probably need to use a computer to help you. I recommend that you begin with a simple word-processing file that identifies the informants and replicates their lists. As you enter the data, review them for consistent spellings and repetitions of terms; word repetition is a real problem in oral listings, but can occur in written lists as well. Our approach has been to eliminate subsequent mentions.

At this point I want to recommend a computer software package called *Anthropac*. It has been designed for just the kinds of exploratory research under consideration in this chapter. For instance, *Anthropac* will take your free-listing data, help you normalize spellings, and perform the necessary computations to generate word frequencies, salience indices, and the like. It also creates matrix files that can be used to perform cluster analysis and multidimensional scaling, both very useful for the understanding of structures in cultural domains. In addition, *Anthropac* has programs for conducting other kinds of domain exploration activities, such as triads testing and pile sorting. *Anthropac* is an excellent tool for the ethnographer concentrating on verbal data collection and analysis.

If you do not have access to *Anthropac* you may complete your analysis of free-listing data with a more generic spreadsheet or database program, or simply do it by hand. The simplest approach is to determine the frequency with which terms are mentioned and use this figure to rank the terms. The most frequently mentioned terms are most salient and are typically the terms that would be examined in greater detail through additional interviewing and general ethnographic observation. If you wish to go a step further, the formula for Smith's S (which combines frequency and order of mention into a single salience index) is as follows:

$$S = \frac{\sum \frac{L-R+1}{L}}{N}$$

where S is the average rank of an item summed across all lists in the sample, weighted by the lengths of the lists in which the item actually occurs; L = the length of a list (the number of items in it), R = the rank of an item in the list; and N = the total number of lists in the sample.

Anthropac will do these calculations for you, but you may wish to see how the different measures affect the ordering of the data. In any event, it is a good idea to take the rankings and create a bar chart so that you can visually inspect the frequency patterns for an "elbow" or break (i.e., the item at which there is a steep drop in the salience ranking). The group of items above the break are usually the ones that will prove most interesting in your further investigations of the cultural significance of the domain.

Once you have ordered the free-list words by frequency of Smith's S, there are a number of things you can do, including some or all of the pattern analyses mentioned above that are available on *Anthropac*. You will probably want to go back to the people who provided you with the data and report to them about what you found. You might also want to go further and have them perform some additional tasks, such as sorts or triads. You may just wish to have people talk about the domain and the words in it. Doing so can give you important insights into further structuring of the domain. As the work of Berlin and Kay showed, most salient terms are often at the top of a taxonomy. The remaining terms in a free-list set are therefore likely to be groupable under the most salient terms as kinds, types, or subtypes within the domain.

A Few Selected Readings for Further Information

Berlin, Brent, and Paul Kay. 1969. *Basic Color Terms*. Berkeley: University of California Press.

Borgatti, Stephen P. 1996. *Anthropac 4.92*. Natick, MA: Analytical Technologies.

Hardin, C. L., and Luisa Maffi, eds. 1997. *Color Categories in Thought and Language.* Cambridge, MA: Cambridge University Press.

Smith, J. Jerome. 1993. Using *Anthropac 3.5* and a Spreadsheet to Compute a Free-list Index. *Cultural Anthropology Methods* 5(3):1–3.

Smith, J. Jerome, Louanna Furbee, Kelly Maynard, Sarah Quick, and Larry Ross. 1995. Salience Counts: A Domain Analysis of English Color Terms. *Journal of Linguistic Anthropology* 5(2):203–216.

Smith, J. Jerome, and Stephen P. Borgatti. 1998. Salience Counts—and So Does Accuracy: Correcting and Updating a Measure for Free-list Item Salience. *Journal of Linguistic Anthropology* 7(2):208–209.

Weller, Susan C., and A. Kimball Romney. 1988. *Systematic Data Collection.* Newbury Park, CA: Sage.

9

Observing a Workplace

Kathryn Borman, Ellen Puccia,
Amy Fox McNulty, & Bill Goddard

A RESEARCH PROJECT

During the 1990s the National Science Foundation (NSF) responded to a general concern among employers about the shortage of highly skilled workers for the nation's expanding high-tech workplace. Whereas prior research had focused on the transition from high school directly into the workplace, the new NSF initiative concentrated on building the curriculum at the level of the community college in order to provide employers with problem-solving technicians who could work well in teams and adapt their skills to challenges in rapidly changing technical workplace settings.

In 1996, the NSF awarded funds to a three-year project, "Addressing National Needs for Skilled Technical Graduates," led by Kathryn Borman at the University of South Florida (USF) and Jeanne Diesen, an independent contractor working with the Indian River Community College (IRCC). The research team was made up of graduate students in applied anthropology at USF, and faculty members and other staff at IRCC. The overarching aim of the research was to determine the core of skills and knowledge that all Associate of Science (A.S.) degree students must possess in order to function in the workplace. We were particularly interested in the so-called "SMET skills" (science, math, engineering, and technology). This common core would then be used to improve the education sought by A.S. students at the community college, allowing for a more efficient and meaningful acquisition of workplace skills. Our study was undertaken as a sort of hybrid, in that it was both a study of high-tech workplaces and workers and also a project designed to inform policy considerations. The location of the study was the central east coast of Florida. Our sample included workers and supervisors in this region in work sites from five industries chosen on the basis of local and national job-growth projections: computer programming and applications; drafting and design; electronics engineering technology; radiography; and respiratory care.

One primary tool for data collection was the workplace observation, a method that has been used in a wide variety of studies in ethnographic research both descriptive and evaluative. Our research design combined the ethnographic methods of workplace observation and interviews with workers and supervisors at key sites with structured surveys administered to the supervisors. We also employed the Experience Sampling Method (ESM), an innovative new methodology that allows for immediate response to surveys at random times of day. Each data-collection strategy provided important information, although for the purposes of this chapter, we will concentrate on data collection by means of workplace observation.

WORKPLACE OBSERVATION AS A TOOL OF ETHNOGRAPHIC RESEARCH

Although we used multiple data-collection methods to address the research questions and identify the common core of SMET skills needed for the workplace, we recognized the importance of broadening the research to include a study of the culture of contemporary technical work. In designing the research tool kit, we therefore determined that observations would provide valuable firsthand knowledge of the workers' jobs, responsibilities, skills, and competencies. Moreover, workplace observations allowed us to understand the work setting and the context of technical work. We were interested in such issues as gender status in the workplace, the structure of management, the transmission of new knowledge, and the role of informal learning in the new technological workplace.

Site-based or contextual skills are essential in the acquisition of new technical knowledge. Contextual knowledge is knowledge that is used in the workplace, and access to such information is very important for workers who want to solve problems efficiently so as to perform their jobs well. Knowledge and skills learned outside the classroom are often imparted through "communities of practice"; in other words, workers learn from others on the job. In addition to the training and preparation A.S.-degree graduates receive at the community college, they continue to learn through informal instruction on the job. Such informal learning is an important part of the ongoing training of technical workers. Because of the wide variety of tasks performed by technical workers and evolving technology, technical workers must constantly update their knowledge and skills.

Observations were essential to the gathering of data about such matters in the workplace. We observed fourteen A.S.-degree graduates in the five selected occupations (three in computer programming and applications, three in drafting and design, two in electronics engineering technology, three in radiography, and three in respiratory care). Because our study involved five researchers in multiple and diverse settings, we had to make sure that everyone followed an observation protocol that was reliable and valid, yet flexible. We wanted to capture both the details of the people's work and the environments in which they worked. We examined the relevant literature, reviewed the research questions, refined the interview protocol and survey, and created our own observation protocol. Our team of researchers needed to make sure that we collected similar data despite the diversity of fields being observed. Our observation protocol contained a list of variables that would be identified at each workplace. These variables included: a map of the work area; census information about co-workers and clients (if applicable); detailed descriptions of the workers' activities; conversations (when possible); approaches to problem solving and decision making; and descriptions of the workplace environment (e.g., gender status, the workplace hierarchy). Observers agreed on a notation system for recording different types of information, distinguishing among observations, conversations, and the observer's own reflections.

The researchers conducted interviews and observations in the same technical field. For example, the researcher who interviewed graduates in drafting and design also conducted the observations of a sample of workers in that field. Each observation lasted between ten and twenty hours and occurred over a two- to four-day period. Observations took place over four months in the summer of 1997. It is important to note that there were several limitations on the observations. For example, some employers in the electronics industry expressed concerns about security, while those in the health fields were mainly concerned about patient confidentiality.

Our observations made it possible for us to identify the skills used by technical workers in carrying out their daily routines. They also allowed us to understand the great importance of informal learning in all five fields. Because the community college was interested in identifying a common core of skills and competencies, it was important to observe the routines of workers and compare their skills across the industries. For example, observations highlighted the importance of social skills such as negotiating and problem solving with the cooperation of co-workers, and the ability to juggle multiple tasks and responsibilities without losing track of the larger context of the job.

One of our key findings—the result mainly of our ethnographic observations—was that women frequently cooperate and work as team members, especially with female co-workers in fields such as radiography and respiratory care, which have a high percentage of female workers. But in fields with a higher percentage of male workers, women may be excluded from acquiring workplace skills, and they may even lose confidence in their abilities to perform even basic tasks.

With regard to the common core of skills, we discovered that thirty-one competencies were identified in all five industries. In addition to the SMET skills, we identified such skills as thinking, employability, interpersonal, and writing/reading skills. Supervisors agreed that their workers needed to possess problem-solving abilities and common sense as well as good work habits, time-management skills, flexibility, and initiative. Workers also need to be able to communicate with people both within and outside of the company. In fact, seventeen of the common core skills are not SMET skills, and of the fourteen SMET skills, seven were mathematical, two were scientific, and five were technological.

Our ethnographic work also allowed both supervisors and workers to make recommendations about how to improve community college education. The most common recommendation was to increase computer training, especially as related to up-to-date software packages relevant to each field of interest. Supervisors and workers also agreed that there is not at present a sufficiently clear emphasis on interpersonal and communications skills in the community college curricula and that students should be trained in the customer orientation of their chosen occupations. As a result of these recommendations, the community college is taking steps to form permanent relationships with the local industries as it makes changes in the A.S. curriculum.

WORKPLACE OBSERVATION: A BRIEF HISTORY

Ethnographies of workplaces based on observational methods go back at least to the 1920s, when a noted study at a Westinghouse plant revealed the potentially reactive nature of conducting such research. In that much-analyzed study, it became clear that the mere presence of the researchers affected the responses of the workers under observation, hence the need, discussed earlier, for using carefully constructed protocols to guide the research.

The liveliest and richest workplace ethnographies are those that focus on the workplace as a community of practice and that emphasize both the importance of interpersonal relations with co-workers and the kinds of tasks undertaken in those contexts. Borman's earlier research on young workers in their first jobs after high school demonstrated the importance of social skills (the capacity to solve problems in and learn through small work groups), just as she found in the later community college study. One influential model of community of practice is that of Jean Lave and her colleagues, who borrow from the traditional relationship between craft apprentices and craft masters and journey workers, who impart the skills of their trade to novices. In such communities, the transmission of skill is dependent on the strength of the social relationships between novice and expert. In its most customary sense, most of this knowledge is transferred verbally and is dependent on interpersonal relations. Like many a traditional society, the workplace community of practice is a kind of oral culture.

Communities of practice serve as the transmission mechanism for workplace knowledge; they are also the repositories of work skills. Within these communities of co-workers, methods of strategizing and problem solving are forged, communicated, negotiated, and learned. It would be misleading, however, to assume that the entire compliment of respiratory workers on a given work shift, for example, automatically constitute a community of practice. Some workers may function outside the community, continually at the periphery. In our observations, temporary or per diem workers were likely to hold such a position, but in a few cases, a committed "temp" might enjoy the benefits of membership in a community of practice.

WORKPLACE OBSERVATION: THE PROCESS

Carrying out a series of workplace observations can contribute to an understanding of not only the skills and competencies required to do a particular job; such activities can also provide a deep understanding of the task structure of jobs—what people do on a daily basis and how what they do is organized and accomplished. With additional effort, the ethnographer can also learn about power relationships—for example, how gender figures in workplace dynamics, an aspect of our project that became increasingly important in understanding high-tech workplaces as settings for the young workers we observed. In carrying out a set of weekly observations over a period of several weeks in multiple workplaces, we followed ten steps, working first individually and then gradually more as a collectivity, pooling information, talking informally about our research experiences, and developing coding rubrics and analytic processes. The ten steps are not discrete items that follow one after the other—many of them must be undertaken simultaneously, and some follow through the entire research process.

The first step is to focus the observation, which enables the observers to capture similar types of information in a systematic manner. At first, we approached our work settings in a manner that allowed us to make general observations of the context and setting for our more focused observations of the technicians, who were our main concern. We gradually centered our observations on the individual worker who was the participant in our research at each of the settings.

It is necessary to create an observation protocol to provide a framework for data collection. An observation protocol should clearly delineate the types of information to be noted (e.g., number of people in the room, interactions, relevant conversations). Our protocol was for the most part an effort to standardize our workplace observations by noting the activities underway at intervals of approximately five to ten minutes throughout the work day. Our observations lasted the full duration of the worker's work day.

As in all research involving human subjects, it is vital to obtain informed consent. Before even beginning the study, researchers should clearly explain the purpose(s) of their project and obtain written permission to observe individuals. Our informed consent form stipulated that any information gathered during the course of study would be maintained in secured files and that pseudonyms would be used to protect workers' identities. As in all the projects in this book, your instructor will help you access your own school's particular informed consent guidelines.

Once a protocol has been developed it must be pilot tested and, if necessary, revised. Our protocol consisted mainly of carrying out a running record of our observations, although other workplace studies have used protocols that took the form of a checklist of the occurrence of particular events and/or behaviors. In either case, it is important to ascertain the validity and reliability of both the tools and your own capacities to capture whatever might be occurring in the setting. A pilot test enables researchers to try out their data-collection instruments with a representative sample of people similar to those who will be involved in the actual study. Following a pilot test, researchers should discuss any complications, problems, or questions that arose and revise the protocol accordingly. Working as a pair or in a team facilitates this process, as a lone individual might take too much for granted and not see all the potential problems.

With the revised protocol in place, it is possible to go ahead and conduct the observations and to do so in a systematic manner. Each observation should be of a specified duration, and the number of such observations should be determined beforehand.

Observers must begin to build rapport with those they will observe as soon as they begin interacting with those workers. Establishing rapport is a process of building a relationship that carries over through the duration of the research. Researchers who come off as impersonal observers or mechanical interviewers are unlikely to build much rapport; they may obtain a certain amount of information, but they will miss the full richness that can come from a true ethnographic immersion in the culture under study.

Observers can play a variety of roles in the research process, with more or less active participation in the setting and with the people depending on the nature of the setting and the constraints of time and other resources on the research. Particularly in a team project, it is important that all members of the team establish and maintain the same role in all the settings under observation. In our project, although we attempted to personalize our presence, we did not become active participants in the work-related activities of the settings.

Type notes immediately following observations while the material is still fresh in mind. Include both objective descriptions as well as subjective reflections on the process in as much detail and with as many nuances as possible.

A codebook should be developed to help researchers examine their notes and classify the information into categories or codes that relate to research questions. By coding data, researchers can look for themes and examine relevant sections of the data. Our codebook was based on several variables, including science skills, math skills, technical skills, and engineering skills. Within each category we further refined the codes to reflect the specific types of skills employed.

Finally, the research team should hold one or more "coding parties" to establish reliability. After completing a codebook, researchers should independently code the same sample of data and then come together to compare their classifications. A "coding party" allows researchers to compare their analyses of data and increase reliability from one rater to another.

YOUR PROJECT

You are to select a workplace to observe, first obtaining permission from the relevant authorities to conduct research there. In your first contact, you should explain that your project is for a class assignment; tell your contact why you chose this place to study and what you hope to learn. Speaking with people or observing in a place that is not public requires informed consent, and you must complete your school's informed-consent form and append it to the report you submit for this project. Your observations should take a minimum of six hours. You may conduct this project either on your own or in pairs.

Your final paper should address the following questions: What workplace did you observe? What did you hope to discover through your observations? (Note that this question requires a very specific answer, not "I want to learn about working in this company.") Describe the physical setting. Report on a census (How many people are there? To what demographic categories—gender, age, ethnicity, etc.—do they seem to belong [that is, you may not have the opportunity to ask each of them individually to verify your hunch]?). Describe the people you see and what they are doing. What do people generally do in this place? Are people interacting with others? Who? How? If they are mostly alone, what are they doing? What is the "tone" of the setting (tense?

serene? exciting?)? How do you know? Do you think that this tone is deliberately set, or did it arise on its own?

Your paper should also provide some information about you as a researcher. Explain why you chose this place. Did you bring any preconceived notions about this place (or others like it) to the observation? If so, were they modified? How? Explain how you went about structuring your observations: What protocol did you use, and how did you develop and pilot test it? What role did you adopt? Why? How did you record notes? How did you code your data for analysis?

Finally, what in general did you learn about the workplace from your observation? Do you have any suggestions to make to the workers or the employers for improving the situation?

A FEW SELECTED READINGS FOR FURTHER INFORMATION

Barley, Stephen R., and Julian Orr. 1997. *Between Craft and Science: Technical Work in U.S. Settings*. Ithaca, NY: Cornell University Press.

Borman, Kathryn M. 1991. *The First "Real" Job: A Study of Young Workers*. Albany: State University of New York Press.

Darrah, Charles. 1994. Skill Requirements at Work. *Work and Occupations* 31(1):68–84.

Lave, Jean, and Etienne Wenger. 1991. *Situated Learning: Legitimate Peripheral Participation*. Cambridge, UK: Cambridge University Press.

Orr, Julian. 1996. *Talking about Machines: An Ethnography of a Modern Job*. Ithaca, NY: ILR Press.

10

Carrying Out a
Structured Observation

Laurie J. Price

A RESEARCH PROJECT

Although it may sometimes seem that ethnographers observe people and behavior just in the act of hanging around, it is sometimes necessary for them to carry out more structured observations in order to answer specific questions. For example, I was involved in a needle hygiene study that sought to gather information about the transmission of HIV/AIDS among injection-drug users. We required very systematic observations of personal risk behaviors. The virus spreads in part when users of illegal drugs use each others' injection syringes, and public health programs needed to know the extent and varieties of needle sharing in order to understand clients' risks and the impact that education and counseling can have on risk-taking behavior.

Ethnographic methods have long been an important part of research on drug-use behavior, perhaps because the activity is covert and researchers are not granted access unless they are around long enough to develop rapport and trust. Ethnographic observation is particularly important when the subject is one about which participants might not be entirely forthcoming when asked questions about their behavior. Structured observations allow the researcher to develop some reasonably objective data to confirm (or perhaps to modify) what people tell us.

I became involved with research on injection behaviors as a member of a research and HIV-prevention program for drug users in northern Arizona: the Flagstaff Multicultural AIDS Prevention Project (FMAPP), which was funded by the National Institute on Drug Abuse. FMAPP collaborated with about twenty other such programs around the country as part of a collaborative agreement. I designed the needle-hygiene study with two other anthropologists within this collaborative arrangement, Stephen Koester and Michael Clatts. We developed the protocol (the formal guidelines for conducting the research) that was used to collect data in seven study sites around the United States. Structured observation was chosen as our primary method partly to ensure that the data from these different sites could be readily compared.

Most of the sites were in large urban areas. Flagstaff, by contrast, is a small town. Even so, over 800 people were clients of FMAPP during the 1990s. These clients took part in a two-session standard education program or a four-session enhanced education/counseling program. They also were offered free HIV testing and counseling. Our research observations were conducted almost entirely with people who had either been or were about to become FMAPP clients. We observed six injection episodes involving a total of twenty-seven individuals.

Our approach had two major aims. First, we needed to observe and record a variety of injection-drug behaviors in groups of people in natural settings and to do so in a systematic way. Second, we needed to take notes on what people said during these episodes, the better to understand how they interact with one another and how they interpret their own risks with regard to HIV. We developed the protocol in order to record: material culture at the scene; background pertinent to the group and its drug use on that occasion; about twenty different specific behaviors; and a small number of direct (verbatim) quotes of what people said.

Needle-related risks include direct re-use of another's syringe, drug management practices (e.g., syringe mixing and syringe-based measurement), and ineffective syringe cleaning practices. Most drug users in northern Arizona fit into one of four types of social patterns, differentiated by their level of openness to new members and the closeness and duration of relationships among group members. To gain a more complete picture of needle use in our community, the study design called for observation in each type of group. Such an approach illustrates an important general principle in structured observation: the researcher often needs to make considered choices about who and where to observe; in other words, it is necessary to devise deliberate sampling strategies.

We learned several important things about needle hygiene as a result of our structured observations. First, we noted that there are two kinds of direct needle sharing: intended and unintended. Direct intended sharing of syringes involves one person deliberately loaning his or her syringe to another and occurred in only two of the six groups we observed. Four people (15% of the total study population) were potentially exposed to the virus in this way. Our observations indicate that unintended direct sharing is the more common method. It would be necessary to confirm these observations by following syringe trajectories over time (i.e., through more than one episode). But based on our single observations, we ascertained that 30–40% of the syringes were "status unknown" (i.e., previously used and not properly cleaned). Most of the participants believed that they were using syringes they themselves had used before, but there was no way to prove this contention since the equipment was not always carefully marked when stored.

All the groups included at least a few FMAPP clients who were known by the researchers to be aware of the risks associated with direct sharing. These people also knew about the observations ahead of time. They therefore had the opportunity to locate their own syringes and thus avoid obvious direct sharing during the observed episode. But over the long run, they could not be assumed to be using similar care in the storage and subsequent usage of the equipment. Unintended direct sharing therefore becomes an important potential source of infection, one that needs to be studied at greater length.

We were also able to observe indirect sharing, which involves the use of common rinse water or cookers. It may also involve the use of one person's syringe as a measuring device for the whole group. A group of people will frequently pool their resources to buy a quantity of heroin, as it is usually cheaper to buy in bulk. It is easier to measure each person's share after the drug is mixed with water and cooked. We observed one episode when a common cooker was used; the first person took up some of the drug in his syringe, but since he was deemed to have taken more than his share, he had to empty some of it back into the cooker. Any blood residue in his syringe from previous injections was therefore mixed with the remaining solution in the cooker. If he had HIV, the other five people in the group would then be exposed to the virus.

Ethnographers recorded other kinds of indirect sharing. For example, one syringe was used to measure water for the group's common cooker. Three syringes were later left floating in one glass of water. The first person to inject returned his syringe to this glass, thus potentially contaminating the other two. Moreover, one group member stored cottons for future use that had been used during injection by another group member; they may have contained blood residue.

One of the most precise parts of our observation protocol involved syringe-cleaning behavior. Bleach is the only substance that really deactivates the HIV virus, so we noted whether people cleaned their syringes and whether they used water, alcohol, bleach, or something else. Even bleach must be left standing for at least sixty seconds to kill the virus. So when people did use bleach, we timed the number of seconds they left it in the syringes.

We found that more often than not, the bleach was left in for only twenty to forty seconds, not long enough for effective decontamination. This finding has clear implications for HIV-prevention programs: clients needed to be taught the sixty-second bleach rule more effectively.

In sum, we documented both intended and unintended direct sharing, as well as the prevalence of indirect sharing, especially when drugs are bought in common. We also documented the inadequacy of syringe-cleaning practices, noting cleaning substances and the frequent time deficits even when people did use bleach. All of these behaviors are associated with potential transmission of HIV (as well as hepatitis). These behaviors need to be specifically addressed in AIDS prevention education and counseling programs for injection-drug users. Structured observations are most useful for documenting behaviors of which people are only partially conscious or about which they have reason to be evasive.

THE STRUCTURED OBSERVATION AS A TOOL OF ETHNOGRAPHIC RESEARCH

Structured observation has been used in ethnographic studies for a variety of purposes, including: characterizing physical locations; understanding the "proxemic spacing" typical of a culture (i.e., how people use spatial arrangements in order to communicate nonverbally); determining the meanings of other forms of nonverbal communication (e.g., eye contact, body language); describing purchasing behaviors; analyzing the components of large and complex natural behavioral settings; describing shifts in group size and composition. Perhaps the most famous and ambitious research project to use structured observations was the Six Cultures Study directed by John and Beatrice Whiting beginning in the 1950s. Twenty-four children were selected in each of six locales (East Africa, Okinawa, Mexico, North India, the Philippines, New England), which were subdivided into behavioral settings (e.g., home, school, playground) where children would typically be found. The activities of the children were observed in each setting during a minimum of fourteen five-minute observation periods. The observers were to record the time and place of the activity, note the persons present, and describe all the stimuli that may have resulted in the observed behavior of the children. The Whitings' aim was to collect structured, systematic data in order to draw reliable conclusions about cultural differences in how children assert dominance, seek attention, initiate play, and reprimand other children.

I also used structured observations in a project I conducted in Ecuador. My focus was on purchasing behaviors of customers in two urban pharmacies. I wanted to document the kinds of prescription drugs bought without a prescription (which turned out to include the antibiotics tetracycline and chloramphenicol, as well as steroids, barbiturates, and clioquinol and dipyrone, drugs banned in most of the industrialized world because they are unsafe). Fifty-one percent of 619 observed sales transactions were for prescription drugs bought without prescriptions. Often as few as two or three capsules of antibiotic were bought in such transactions. I was also interested in describing the ways in which customers sought out drugstore clerks for medical advice.

Richard Lee used a structured-observation protocol in his widely read ethnographic study of the !Kung (Ju'/hoansi) San of southern Africa. His focus was on sources of food and composition of diet, and so he measured such things as: the distance people walked from camp to the gathering or hunting sites; the weight of nuts collected or animals killed per hour of labor; camp members' average caloric intake from both plant and animal sources; the number of different foods consumed; and social relationships of those who shared food of different types.

THE STRUCTURED OBSERVATION: THE PROCESS

The first step in designing a structured-observation study is to decide what specific questions you want to answer. It is usually a good idea to use this data-collection technique with a topic with which you are already somewhat familiar, so that you will have a reasonably good idea of which variables are important and which measures of those variables will be most pertinent to the group under observation. When we drafted the protocol for the needle-hygiene study, for example, all three of us had prior experience in qualitative research with drug users. We selected the following items for observation based on those prior exposures:

- Date/time in/time out
- Name(s) of observer(s)
- Setting and context (e.g., house; car; shooting gallery)
- Participants (using ID numbers or pseudonyms)
- Descriptions of participants (age, ethnicity, sexual orientation, social relationships with each other)
- Chronology of events
- Description of injection equipment participants come in with: Are the syringes new, used, rented, or bought from someone at the site? Are cookers individual or common? Is rinse water individual or common? Are cottons individual or common?
- Drugs injected: Which ones? How were they procured?

- Description of sequential order of participants' needle-sharing; from whom do they borrow (i.e., social relationship)?; statements (if any) regarding their reasons for sharing
- Is there a pile of syringes at any point?
- Cleaning of syringes: With what? How long (carefully timed)?
- Record of other verbal interactions among participants (get verbatim quotes whenever possible).

Many of these items are standard for ethnographic observation, but note that we made sure to use ID numbers to preserve confidentiality. The observation of social relations among members of the group was particularly important for our purposes, as were the questions focused on the material culture (i.e., the injection equipment, its preparation and treatment) and the social relations that revolved around those items. Questions about cleaning the syringes were necessary in order to make recommendations about public health: water, alcohol, and bleach are commonly used to clean equipment, although only bleach will actually kill the HIV virus, and then only if it sits in the syringe for at least sixty seconds. We therefore used our watches to time exactly how many seconds the syringes were cleaned.

Verbal behaviors can be an important part of what you decide to include in a structured observation protocol. Because you are writing notes on so many different aspects of the situation, however, you probably will need to make a decision about what kinds of statements are most worthy of being recorded. After all, it takes some time to write down even a few sentences verbatim. A few pithy quotes are often worth as much as half a page of general notes on topics people talked about. In our protocol, we decided to try to record what people said about the drugs, about the drug equipment and how to handle it, and about HIV/AIDS.

The biggest problem in conducting structured observations is often information overload. In our project, the groups could be fairly large (five to seven people) and the action unfolded at a rapid pace (especially during the injection phase); it was a challenge to observe and record all the variables we had identified on our protocol. One solution to this problem was to have each observation conducted by a team of ethnographers; the researchers were positioned in different parts of the room. We undoubtedly missed some things, although certainly not as many as would have been the case with a solitary researcher.

Another potential problem in a project such as ours is cross-site consistency. Although all the ethnographers in all the seven sites were using the same protocol, it was not always possible for them to interpret the variables in the same way. Observers, in fact, varied in how much detail they recorded and in how much background information they collected.

A third issue has to do with the need to conduct some interviewing, as observation alone does not always provide all the information needed for a correct interpretation of the behaviors in question. We tried to ask questions that elicited contextual information, the better to understand what was going on at this particular time in this particular setting. Some background information can be collected at the beginning of the observation, and some questions designed to clarify what just happened are most appropriately left to the end. But the main part of the behavior should be allowed to flow without the researchers' intervention.

YOUR PROJECT

Food is loaded with cultural meanings, and people have a lot to say about what they prefer to eat and what it means to them. But food consumption also calls for observational methods. While not covert in the same way that drug use is, food consumption is often the result of unconscious cues, and our ways of talking about it may be colored, and hence obscured, by our notions of what is socially acceptable. Therefore, your assignment is to observe multiple people eating at a fast-food restaurant. Your main research questions will be: a) What are the food choices that people are actually making? b) How much of their daily caloric and fat consumption do these choices entail? c) Although we call it "fast food," how fast do people actually eat in such places? d) Do customers use these outlets to socialize with others (as opposed to just eating)? e) Do they seem to be enjoying themselves?

To carry out this research, you must first devise an observation protocol. It will probably include many of the same variables noted on our needle-hygiene study protocol (e.g., date, location, time in/out, ethnographic observer(s), setting and context, chronology of events). Each person observed should be assigned either a letter or a pseudonym to preserve confidentiality and should be described in terms of gender, estimated age, ethnicity, probable social relationships with others at the table, and body shape/weight. A small sketch of how the people are arranged at the table will be useful in understanding your notes on group interaction.

If you are working alone, your protocol should be made up primarily of the starred items below; if you are working as a team, you may include other items as time permits. Suggested points to observe:

*• What items are bought? Who did the purchasing? Did everyone stand in line together, or did one person buy everything to bring back to the table?

*• What are the food choices of each person in the group?

*• How much time does a group spend, from the moment they come in the door (include both standing in line waiting for their order and then at the table)? Note that this process should be timed with a watch, at least in minutes, if not in seconds.

• Is food choice a focus of discussion between adults and children, or among adults themselves? (Note that it may or may not be possible to hear such verbal interaction; observation in a public place is taken for granted, but it is just common courtesy to avoid obvious eaves-dropping.) Are toys or other promotional items part of the choices being made?

*• What is the caloric and fat content of the items? (Many fast food restaurants now post these measures. Try to choose a restaurant that does so.)

• Are people sharing their food? If so, who is sharing with whom?

*• What is the nature of the social interaction of groups eating together?

• How much eye contact is there? (This variable could also be timed, if it seems important to you to do so.)

• How would you characterize the tone of voice (pleasant, excited, angry, etc.)? Is anyone eating in silence? (This variable should be sampled at least three or four times during each group's meal, at regularly spaced intervals of, say, five minutes.)

• Who is doing most of the talking, and who is less talkative? (Remember to use the ID or pseudonym.)

*• Does anyone go back for more food? What items do they get? (Add any such additions to your calorie/fat inventory.)

• What reaction, if any, is there to someone going back for more?

• What kind of mood does the group appear to be in when they exit the restaurant?

• Do they take any food with them? If so, what?

• Do they clear their places? Who in the group does so?

Once you have selected your variables, type them up as a formal protocol. A notebook is useful for recording notes and maps of the observation site. As in the needle-hygiene study, your analysis will include both qualitative characterizations and quantitative data. When you have finished your analysis, you should be able to draw some conclusions about fast-food chains and how they relate to both food consumption and the social interactions centered on food.

A FEW SELECTED READINGS FOR FURTHER INFORMATION

Lee, Richard B. 1993. *The Dobe !Kung*. New York: Holt, Rinehart and Winston.

Price, Laurie J. 1989. In the Shadow of Biomedicine: Self-medication in Two Ecuadorian Pharmacies. *Social Science and Medicine* 28(9):905–915.

Whiting, John W. M., Irvin L. Child, and William W. Lambert. 1966. *Field Guide for the Study of Socialization*. New York: Wiley.

11

Designing a Questionnaire for Cross-Cultural Research

Roberta D. Baer & Susan C. Weller

A RESEARCH PROJECT

In 1989, Roberta Baer, Susan Weller, Lee Pachter, and Robert Trotter were attending the annual meetings of the Society for Applied Anthropology, where they discovered that they had all done separate studies of the folk illness *empacho*, which is characterized by gastrointestinal symptoms and is common in Latino populations. Trotter had studied *empacho* among Mexican-Americans; Baer's research was in Mexico itself. Pachter and associates did research in Puerto Rico, and Weller and associates focused on Guatemala. The four anthropologists realized, however, that since they had used different data-collection techniques in their separate studies, it was difficult to compare their findings. They could not even determine definitively whether *empacho* was the same syndrome in all these populations. They therefore decided to construct and administer a single questionnaire that could be used in all four research sites. They were ultimately able to conclude that there was indeed a core of beliefs about susceptibility, causes, symptoms, and treatments that characterized *empacho* in different places.

That experience led to a series of cross-cultural studies of illnesses, both those recognized by the biomedical establishment and those defined mainly in the experiences of everyday, non-professional people ("folk" illnesses). Their research dealt with AIDS, diabetes, colds, asthma, *nervios, caida de mollera, susto,* and *mal de ojo.* These illnesses were selected because they represent a range of conditions among Latin American populations. Studies initially concentrated on four such populations. In the United States, interviews were conducted with Mexican-Americans in Edinburg, Texas, a largely Hispanic town in an agricultural region of the lower Rio Grande Valley along the U.S.-Mexico border. There were also interviews with Puerto Ricans in Hartford, Connecticut, a medium-sized city in the northeast U.S. that has a population that is approximately one-third Hispanic. Outside the U.S., interviews were conducted in Guadalajara, a large industrialized city in central Mexico; residents of Guadalajara are from both rural and urban backgrounds and are predominantly *mestizo* (Spanish speakers who do not claim affiliation with an indigenous group). The fourth field site was in Guatemala, among Spanish-speaking *ladinos* (a local term equivalent to *mestizo* in Mexico) in four rural villages on the agricultural Pacific coastal plain in the department of Esquintla.

Although slight differences were expected in these various Hispanic populations, the researchers decided to do some additional interviews among middle-class Americans of predominantly northern European origin, mainly to add a truly cross-cultural dimension to the conclusions. These interviews (dealing only with AIDS and the common cold) were conducted in Tampa, a medium-sized city in west central Florida.

Our first concern in designing these linked studies was to create interview materials that were truly comparable, even though they were to be administered in communities with different demographic and cultural characteristics. The interview locations were selected for their socioeconomic, historical, and ethnic differences. Interviewing and informant selection took place in two stages. First, a "convenience sample" of twenty women was selected at each Latino site for open-ended, descriptive interviewing. A "convenience sample," as the name implies, is simply a number of people who are available and amenable to being interviewed; the purpose at this point is simply to test the interview questionnaire, not to reach any generalizable conclusions, which would require a more nearly representative sample. When it came time to identify those representative samples, it was necessary to randomize the selection of informants. In Guatemala, the communities were small enough so that a simple strategy of randomization could be used: households were selected from the center to the periphery (to capture the range of social-class variation) in each of the four villages. At other sites, however, a two-stage random-sampling design was used. First, a sampling unit (e.g., a census tract or a neighborhood) was selected. Then, an actual city block was selected, and households on the block were approached for interviewing. In Edinburg, the entire city was sampled from the census tracts. In Hartford, interviews were conducted in the census tracts with the highest concentration of Puerto Ricans. In Guadalajara, sampling focused on three neighborhoods, representing the social and economic variation in the city: middle class, working class, and poor. In Tampa, interviews were conducted in two middle-income census tracts.

Our main interest was in beliefs among Latinos. In both Edinburg and Hartford, we relied on people's self-identification as either Mexican-American or Puerto Rican, respectively. We preferred to interview adults (who would have more experience with the selected illnesses), and usually focused on women, who are typically the household members with the most responsibility for health care. Interviews were conducted by local interviewers fluent in the local dialect. In Texas and Connecticut, Spanish or a combination of Spanish and English was used, according to the preference of the respondent. In Tampa, interviews were conducted by graduate students as part of a class project.

Open-ended, descriptive interviews with a few key informants at each site were used to develop questionnaires. Data were gathered on the perceived causes, symptoms, and treatment of each illness; we used a "free-listing" technique (i.e., we asked the respondents to list as many causes, symptoms, and treatments as they knew about, rather than restricting them to a list of choices pre-set by the research team). Items that were listed in at least 10% of each sample were included in the structured questionnaires, along with additional symptoms listed in the Cornell Medical Index and some concepts that had been reported by ethnographic researchers working on other projects. We made sure to record and use verbatim responses in the informants' language in preparing the questionnaires (rather than paraphrases, which might have introduced unwarranted interpretation into the process).

A true-false questionnaire was developed for each of the illnesses in the study. Each instrument had an average of 130 questions about possible causes, symptoms, and treatments. Each questionnaire also included basic demographic data on the respondents, as well as questions about personal experiences with the illness. Each questionnaire was translated into the form of Spanish or English spoken at each site. Since free-listing interviews had preceded the creation of a formal questionnaire, we had the most salient items for each site, and since most items were obtained verbatim from each site in Spanish, most of those items were modified only minimally for use at all four sites. In general, the adequacy of the translation (Spanish to Spanish) was verified by reviewing all the questions, one by one, with two local interviewers.

THE QUESTIONNAIRE AS A TOOL OF CROSS-CULTURAL ETHNOGRAPHIC RESEARCH: A BRIEF OVERVIEW

Anthropology has always been interested in cross-cultural comparisons, but for the most part researchers have had to rely on data collected by different scholars, using different methods, at different points in time. A more modern approach to cross-cultural research involves the attempt to standardize the process, making sure that a group of researchers will be using the same instrument in the same way in order to elicit truly comparable information from informants in various research sites. A questionnaire is often the most efficient tool for data collection in this context, since it minimizes (although it cannot eliminate completely) the subjective variation that might be introduced in other forms of ethnographic research. A good questionnaire from an anthropological perspective is one that grows directly out of a more broadly based ethnographic understanding of the community in which it is to be administered. The anthropological purpose would be defeated were the questionnaire to be devised by the researchers in their offices, and then taken out to the field. Rather, the questionnaire is designed only after considerable ethnographic exposure to the people and the settings to be surveyed.

Using standardized questionnaires as the basis of cross-cultural research requires that the questionnaire be designed so that the same question is asked in a meaningful way in each population under study. The questions may have to be re-phrased so that they are understandable to people of different ethnic and linguistic backgrounds, even though they are tapping into the same basic body of knowledge.

THE ETHNOGRAPHIC QUESTIONNAIRE: THE PROCESS

Our research project encountered a number of important issues in the process of designing an effective questionnaire suitable for cross-cultural research; although the details are, of course, specific to our particular research settings, they illustrate problems that are of concern to any researchers who use this data-collection technique.

Perhaps the most basic issue is one of translation. In our case, even though virtually all our informants spoke Spanish, there were discernible regional variations in the use of that language. The problem, to be sure, is magnified in cross-cultural research in which completely different languages are in use. For example, our questionnaire relating to the illness known as *mal de ojo* ("evil eye") included a question stated (in English) as the somewhat puzzling, "Does sweeping a person with a big pepper help treat *mal de ojo*?" and (in Spanish) as the no less odd, "Para tratar mal de ojo, se le pasa el enfermo con un chile." The item was included because in the original free list from Guatemala, *pimienta gorda* had been a frequent response. The person who created the draft questionnaire, however, was not Guatemalan, but a Mexican-American from Texas, and she interpreted *pimienta* ("pepper" in English) as the familiar Mexican-American *chile*. When *chile* was translated back into English, it became "big pepper." When Baer tried to use the questionnaire at her site in Guadalajara, she quickly realized that it made no sense in either Mexican Spanish or in English. From prior experience conducting fieldwork in Guatemala, she intuited that what had been intended was allspice (*pimienta gorda*, or "fat pepper," in Guatemalan Spanish). She was unsure of how to render allspice into Mexican Spanish until she searched a local supermarket and found a jar labeled *pimienta dulce* ("sweet pepper").

We initially assumed that the preferred language in south Texas would be Spanish, and had prepared a locally acceptable Spanish version of each question. As it turned out, they preferred to use English for most of their interviews. A problem, however, emerged on the *mal de ojo* questionnaire regarding the use of *barridas* as a treatment. The word is commonly translated as "sweeping" (in the sense of a ritualized action that is part of a folk-healing process), but the south Texas respondents did not recognize the English word in this context. So although the rest of the questionnaire was administered in English, we had to keep the Spanish word *barridas* to describe this particular treatment.

One item used on a number of questionnaires dealt with the role of drinking unboiled water as a cause of illness. The Spanish version of this question administered in Guatemala and Mexico made complete sense; in those areas, most tap water is not safe to drink unless it is boiled. The English version of the question administered in south Texas also made sense, as that population was familiar with the problem of unsafe tap water through contact with family members on the Mexican side of the border. When, however, the question was pre-tested in Tampa, where most people drink the municipally processed tap water, it proved confusing. We re-worded it to read "Can drinking unboiled or impure water cause this illness?"

Slang usage of certain terms was a factor in the revision of one of the questions on the English version of the AIDS questionnaire administered in Tampa. The original English question was, "With AIDS, does a person want to eat sweet things?" In some gay populations, however, this question would have had a sexual connotation, and so we re-worded it as, "With AIDS, does a person want to eat or crave sweet things or sweet foods?"

Moving interview materials through different languages—or even different dialects of the same language—can be difficult. Cross-cultural psychologists have probably written the most about these issues, as they are central to cross-cultural testing. A key issue in any interviewing process is that the questions must be interpreted in the same way by all informants. The best way to begin to create comparable interview materials is to begin with open-ended or free-listed interviews to collect salient, verbatim responses. Incorporation of those responses or themes into more structured interview materials ensures that locally relevant themes are used and are couched in the local language. The free-listing interviews should be used to elicit clear, understandable items that, when repeated to others, are interpreted in the same way. Incorporation of these verbatim responses simply avoids many problems inherent in working with multiple groups.

Once questions are written, their "interpretability" can be tested. During a set of pilot interviews (done with individuals or in groups), respondents may be asked to respond to questions and to "think out loud" about what the question means, what possible answers might be, and how they arrive at a response. The goal is to modify questions so that each and every one is interpreted in the same way by each and every informant.

Cross-cultural psychologists recommend that translation adequacy be achieved through the use of two full translation loops. In other words, the material is translated from the original language to the second and then back again. Two pairs of translators should go through this process, and the results should be compared. The double translation in and out of the source language at each loop helps ensure that concepts can, in fact, move between the two languages.

In the course of developing nine questionnaires of 125–130 questions each, we were able to correct most problems with questions during the initial open-ended interviews, although a few slipped by and were not corrected until the final version of the structured questionnaire was prepared. In a few instances, the problems were not even evident until data analysis had begun. Nevertheless, we do not believe that these problems are so numerous as to discourage others from undertaking questionnaire-based cross-cultural research.

YOUR PROJECT

You (working independently or as part of a team) are to select a topic that is appropriate to study in populations of different cultural backgrounds. For example, you might want to learn more about family, diet, work, or other aspects of life that are found in every culture. Make up at least ten questions in English that address your chosen topic. Using a "convenience sample," ask informants to list all the things they can (free-listing technique). You might perhaps ask someone to list all the foods that might be eaten at a morning meal. Be careful to phrase questions so that they request information, and are not answerable with a simple "yes" or "no." Be sure to get clarification on all responses, so that another informant might know exactly what was meant by the reply. Construct a true/false questionnaire based on the items that show up most frequently in these open-ended interviews.

Find at least two different cultural groups in which to administer the questionnaire. (Depending on the size of your project team, you can expand the number of groups to be surveyed.) Try to work with groups that contrast with regard to ethnicity, social class, educational level, age, gender, or some other recognizable demographic factor. Unless you are fluent in other languages, it might be more efficient if you can find contrasting groups composed of speakers of English. Identify at least five people from each group to whom you will administer your questionnaire. With such a very small sample, you can come up with suggestive trends in need of more comprehensive research; you cannot establish general patterns in any conclusive way.

Alternatively, take an interview that has already been standardized and administered in some population, and check to see whether it is meaningful in a local population not part of the original administration. For example, Baer took a survey widely used by mental-health professionals to assess the level of psychological problems among populations in the United States, and gave it to Mexican and Mexican-American farmworkers in Florida. She found that their responses regarding symptoms would have been interpreted by clinical psychologists as signs of depression, although the people themselves understood their condition as resulting from exhaustion due to hard physical work. You can do a similar exercise by taking a standard survey and administering it to several representatives of a local population. When you do so, make sure that you get, in addition to the answers to the questions themselves, explanations of what the respondents thought the questions meant, and why they answered the way they did.

In either case, your report should include a brief summary of your findings (i.e., what did you learn from the responses to the questionnaire?), although the focus should be on the process: write about how you developed the survey instrument, and discuss the ways in which it was understood (or not) by everyone to whom it was administered. Which questions need to be re-worded, and how? To what extent did you encounter any of the translation problems discussed above?

A FEW SELECTED READINGS FOR FURTHER INFORMATION

Baer, Roberta D. 1989. Lead-Based Remedies for *Empacho*: Patterns and Consequences. *Social Science and Medicine* 29(12):1373–1379.

———. 1996. Health and Mental Health among Mexican-American Migrant Workers: Implications for Survey Research. *Human Organization* 55:58–66.

Baer, Roberta D., and Susan C. Weller. 1999. Beliefs about AIDS in Five Latin and Anglo-American Populations. *Anthropology and Medicine* 6(1):13–29.

———. 1999. Cross-Cultural Perspectives on the Common Cold. *Human Organization* 58(3):251–260.

Brislin, Richard. 1986. The Wording and Translation of Research Instruments. In *Field Methods in Cross-Cultural Research*, ed. Walter J. Lonner and John W. Berry, 137–164. Beverly Hills, CA: Sage.

Pachter, Lee, B. Bernstein, and A. Osorio. 1992. *Empacho* in a Mainland Puerto Rican Population. *Medical Anthropology* 13(4):285–299.

Trotter, Robert. 1985. *Greta* and *Azarcon*. *Human Organization* 44(1):64–72.

Trotter, Robert, Susan C. Weller, and Roberta D. Baer. Consensus Theory Model of AIDS/SIDA in Four Latino Populations. *AIDS Education and Prevention* 11(5):414–426.

Weller, Susan C., and Roberta D. Baer. 1999. Latino Beliefs about Diabetes. *Diabetes Care* 22(5):722–728.

Weller, Susan C., Lee Pachter, Robert Trotter, and Roberta D. Baer. 1993. *Empacho* in Four Latino Groups. *Medical Anthropology* 15:109–136.

Weller, Susan C., T. K. Ruebush, and R. Klein. 1990. An Epidemiological Description of a Folk Illness. *Medical Anthropology* 13:19–31.

12

Working with Numerical Data

Martha W. Rees

A RESEARCH PROJECT

Introductory courses in the social sciences sometimes leave students with the impression that there is a sharp and permanent divide between ethnographic data (which are presumed to be subjective, impressionistic, and somehow "soft") and numerical data (which are thought to be objective, scientific, and "hard"). But in fact most social scientists need to learn how to work comfortably with both kinds of data, and certain kinds of research questions actually call for a creative combination of the two. For example, I have been involved in a study of the growing Hispanic presence in Atlanta, and at one point a question arose as to the number of immigrant Mexican women in the population. Since there were no published census figures that could supply an easy answer, our research team used a combination of ethnographic means in order to come up with some workable estimated numbers.

We know that the number of Hispanic women in the U.S. labor market is on the rise, but the category "Hispanic" includes non-Mexicans and non-

123

immigrants. Definitions of ethnic categories are political in nature. Decisions about who is Hispanic influence: school budgets; the availability of English-as-a-Second-Language (ESL) training; the allocation of resources for bilingual education and translation services; and the languages in which ballots and driver's license exams are printed. In the United States, native-born citizens (some of whom have roots in the region that go back to before there even was a United States) who speak Spanish or have Spanish surnames are typically lumped together with more recent migrants from the Americas and other parts of the Spanish-speaking world. Given the broadness of the category, we have to take published figures with a grain of salt. So when we read that the participation of "Hispanic women" in the labor force increased 14% between 1960 and 1980, we must ask whether this increase is due to immigration or to the presence of more U.S. citizens of Hispanic descent entering the work force.

Within the larger category of "Hispanics," there is a demographically important sub-category of people of Mexican heritage. We know that the number of Mexican migrants to the U.S. has been increasing, but information about the characteristics of that migrant population is sketchy. And information about women within that migrant population is still harder to obtain. Most of the research on Mexican migration has focused on males who leave their homeland to work and then send remittances back to their families. Scholars working with this "push" theory of migration assume that male migration is an individual income-maximizing strategy. The real situation, however, is almost certainly more complex. For one thing, women who stay at home are not simply sitting idle waiting for remittance payments; most women work for pay, and their incomes actually make it possible for the men to migrate. Moreover, remittances do form the third largest source of foreign exchange in Mexico and cannot be underestimated as an important factor in people's decisions about earning a living; but it is clear that there is increasing female migration as well—women are entering the U.S. either as individuals or to join husbands, and most of them become part of the work force as they do so.

The pace of Mexican migration to the U.S. increased in the 1980s, and this new wave of migrants seems to have included more families and more single women. Conditions in Mexico contributed to this upsurge in migration: in 1986 the price of petroleum fell and Mexico, for the first time in three decades, suffered negative economic growth and triple-digit inflation. One result of this economic crisis was lower wages; indeed, wages in Mexico fell to their lowest point in 1987. Recovery of international confidence came at the cost of salary increases and social subsidies. Economic conditions worsened for the working and middle classes and the potential for social unrest increased. The crisis encouraged both males and females to move from Mexico to the United States, where wages were higher.

At the same time, the U.S. economy was undergoing changes of its own. U.S. companies were moving production to lower-wage areas, including Mexico, and the labor market in the U.S. itself became increasingly service-oriented. But there was still a need for cheap, low-skilled labor, and many employers seemed to prefer illegal migrants for such tasks, since undocumented laborers tend to be more compliant, living as they do in constant fear of deportation.

In sum, Mexican migration to the United States can only be explained in terms of multiple local, national, and global factors. Female migration also requires a multi-dimensional explanation; it must also take into account household characteristics and women's activities in Mexico. Entire households may be more likely to migrate if there is work for both spouses, which seems to be the case in Atlanta, which has a high demand for workers in meatpacking and domestic services.

Atlanta is the largest urban center in the southeastern United States, and since the 1980s the region has undergone profound social, cultural, and demographic change. The region had historically been home to two main ethnic groups: African-Americans and European-Americans. In the 1970s and 1980s, however, more than 10,000 migrants and refugees from Vietnam arrived, changing not only the ethnic make-up, but also the political, economic, and social relations of the region. The Hispanic population of Georgia has also grown, especially in the metropolitan area of Atlanta, made up of Fulton, DeKalb, Gwinnett, Cobb, and Cherokee counties. Hispanics now form the largest non-traditional minority group, growing in numbers from 30,000 in 1982 to over 110,000 in 1992, a 260% increase in ten years. Between 1992 and 1996, the Hispanic population of the Atlanta metro area grew to over 231,619, an increase of 100% in just six years. Four percent of this population (9,571 individuals) are children in school whose first language is Spanish.

The increase in the number of Hispanics in the southeastern U.S. indicates that there is a specific demand for their labor, due in part to construction associated with the 1996 Olympic Games, but more to the growth of industries such as meatpacking, carpet and textile manufacture, and services in homes, gardens, and restaurants.

This Hispanic population is, by common agreement, undercounted in census figures. In order to find out about Mexican women (a sub-set of a sub-category within that larger population), it is necessary to estimate. Our research team therefore used whatever census figures were available, but supplemented them with survey data and ethnographic data. The survey data were collected in the course of interviews with both male and female Mexican migrants in Atlanta in 1998 (T. Danyael Miller and Mariposa Arillo, research scholars at Agnes Scott College, helped collect the data), and the ethnographic information resulted from interviews extending from 1993 to 2000.

WORKING WITH NUMERICAL DATA: THE PROCESS

I interviewed intake personnel at health, religious, and social-service agencies about the percentage of Hispanics who are Mexican. Ethnographic data from social-service centers that deal with Hispanics indicate that about 90% of Hispanics are Mexican. Thinking it best to err on the side of caution, I used the figure of 80% as a working estimate. So if there are, by official count, 231,619 Hispanics in the Atlanta metropolitan area, there should be 185,295 Mexicans. Of these, how many are women? The answer is not so easily ascertained. Although historically the majority of Mexican immigrants have been male, the situation is certainly changing, and so historical estimates may no longer be useful. Many Mexicans are undocumented, and women in particular seem to enter the U.S. without papers, a situation that makes them all the more difficult to count. Since our research team lacked the resources to carry out a large-scale survey of all women in the metropolitan area to determine how many are Mexican, we designed a survey questionnaire that asked for basic demographic and household information and applied it to an opportunity sample of Mexican women in the metropolitan area. We interviewed forty-nine women in the spring of 1998 at the Mexican consulate, at a social-service center, at a local Catholic mission, and elsewhere as the opportunity arose. We found many more women than expected—at a Catholic mass, more than half were women (compared, however, to 90% in Mexico). There are lots of Mexican women (*mexicanas*) working in restaurants, in domestic service, in meatpacking companies, in carpet factories, and in hotels. How could we get at a reasonably accurate number?

We started with some data that we actually did have. We knew, for example, that in 1996 there were at least 9,571 children in public schools whose first language is Spanish. If the proportion of Mexicans in the larger Hispanic population is the same for children as for adults (80%, as noted above), then there are 7,656 Mexican children in school. Women are obviously linked to their children, and we thought we could calculate the number of women on the basis of the average number of children that each woman has. The forty-nine women represented in our survey had a total of twenty-six children of school age (i.e., between the ages of six and eighteen). Each woman therefore had an average of .53 children. So if one child represents two women, the 7,656 Mexican children represent 14,445 Mexican women. I concluded that there were therefore about 14,000 Mexican women in Atlanta in early 1999. (The continued rapid growth in the number of Mexicans in the metropolitan area means that this figure must be revised upward.)

This estimate must be used with some caution. First, it is based on an opportunity sample, not a random sample. We do not know the size (or even the location) of the entire population of Mexican women, so we cannot draw a statistically accurate sample. By sampling different venues, we tried to cover different types of Mexican women (those who come to clinics with their children, to the consulate for official documents, and so forth), but again we do not know the characteristics of the population as a whole, so that we can only guess as to the degree to which the women we interviewed were representative. Since our survey was carried out in social-service agencies, it may be biased toward working-class migrants, although all kinds of Mexicans come to the consulate, for example. It may well be that the results of an opportunity sample are as accurate as those of a truly random sample, but we cannot count on such a convergence. Another problem with the survey is that it may overestimate the number of children in school. Many Mexican children drop out between tenth and eleventh grade. Moreover, some of the women may have children (especially older ones) back in Mexico.

Despite these problems, it was necessary to work with our estimate. More and more *mexicanas* are migrating to the U.S. in general, and to Atlanta in particular. Atlanta seems to be a destination of choice for younger women who follow their husbands within a few years of their marriage and his initial migration. If the 1999 estimate of 14,000 Mexican women in Atlanta is even roughly correct, then they were still a small portion of the Mexican population of 185,000, which itself was 80% of the total Hispanic population. But we have every reason to believe that women are systematically undercounted, a problem that has only increased since 1996 when schools were no longer required to collect and report data about Spanish-speaking students—a main source of the inferences in our estimate. The presence of Mexican women in Atlanta obviously affects the Mexican community, social services, employment, and culture—factors that will become ever more important as the numbers continue to grow. It is to our advantage to develop more accurate ways of counting their numbers. Until then, estimates based on ethnographic data collection will have to do.

YOUR PROJECT

In addition to undocumented immigrants, there are many undercounted, almost hidden populations in our midst. For example, how would you count the homeless, HIV-positive people, gays and lesbians, or drug users? Getting at least some estimates for any of these groups would have a real impact on the nature and delivery of social and health services. Select one such population in your local area. It is probably best to work as a team, whose assignment is to predict changes in demand for health or other social services as a result of changes in an undercounted, underserved population. Using a combination of published census or other official figures and ethnographic surveys and/or interviews as we did in the Atlanta study, come up with a working estimate of the number of people in your selected population. Your report should also include a discussion of the pros and cons of the process, particularly with regard to the reliability and validity of the selected measures.

A FEW SELECTED READINGS FOR FURTHER INFORMATION

Babbie, Earl. 1994. *The Practice of Social Research*. Belmont, CA: Wadsworth.

Bustamante, Jorge, Clark W. Reynolds, and Raúl A. Hinojosa Ojeda. 1992. *U.S.–Mexico Relations: Labor Market Interdependences*. Stanford, CA: Stanford University Press.

Castells, Manuel. 1980. *The Economic Crisis and American Society*. Princeton, NJ: Princeton University Press.

Collins, Jane. 1988. *Unseasonal Migrations: The Effects of Rural Labor Scarcity in Peru*. Princeton, NJ: Princeton University Press.

Cornelius, Wayne A. 1991. Los Migrantes de la Crisis: The Changing Profile of Mexican Migration to the U.S. In *Social Responses to Mexico's Economic Crisis of the 1980s*, ed. Mercedes González de la Rocha and Agustín Escobar Latapí, 155–192. San Diego: University of California, San Diego, Center for U.S.–Mexican Studies.

Donato, Katherine. 1992. Current Trends and Patterns of Female Migration: Evidence from Mexico. *International Migration Review* 27(4):748–771.

Hondagneu-Sotelo, Pierrette. 1994. *Gendered Transitions: Mexican Experiences of Immigration*. Berkeley: University of California Press.

Jenkins, J. Craig. 1977. Push/Pull in Recent Mexican Migration to the U.S. *International Migration Review* 11:178–189.

Massey, Douglas S., Joaquín Arango, Graeme Hugo, Ali Kouaouci, Adela Pellerino, and J. Edward Taylor. 1994. An Evaluation of International Migration Theory: The North American Case. *Population and Development Review* 20(4):899–951.

Stier, Haya, and Marta Tienda. 1992. Family, Work, and Women: The Labor Supply of Hispanic Immigrant Wives. *International Migration Review* 26(4):1291–1313.

13

Constructing a Virtual Ethnography

S. Elizabeth Bird & Jessica Barber

A RESEARCH PROJECT

For some years now Bird has been studying the role of the media in the contemporary United States. Today we live in a media-saturated world; the media do not merely affect culture—they are actually embedded in our culture. They provide us with many of our shared cultural references, and it is through the media that American culture is moving so quickly across the globe.

As an anthropologist, Bird's main research focus is not on the effects of the media—which are difficult, if not impossible, to measure—but on how people relate to various media. She has studied the audiences of supermarket tabloids and television news programming and explored how people respond to media images of American Indians. In the past, she used familiar methods, such as observations, in-depth interviews, and focus groups, to investigate how people use the media in their everyday lives. But the research on representations of American Indians led her into a new kind of media ethnography.

Bird had written an article about how White and American Indian viewers responded to the television series *Dr. Quinn, Medicine Woman*, which regularly featured Cheyenne characters. She concluded that White viewers tended to accept the rather stereotypical portrayal of the Cheyenne, precisely because it fit with the way mainstream culture had come to understand how Indians *should* behave. Indian viewers, on the other hand, found these same stereotypes demeaning.

Bird was surprised one day to receive an e-mail from a woman who had read her article and who explained that she was a member of an e-mail discussion list devoted to *Dr. Quinn*; she requested permission to post the article for the members' comments. Bird agreed and then subscribed to the list in order to read and respond to those comments. Fascinated by the careful, lengthy discussions that followed, Bird began to realize that this electronic fan group could provide a way to understand how at least some people use the Internet both to discuss their favorite television show and to communicate in the most basic sense—to make connections with people that went beyond the context of the show. Bird began several years of "virtual ethnography," in which she observed and participated on the discussion list, interviewed members, and asked them to respond to her interpretations of their community. She learned a great deal, not only about the role of the Internet in media fan culture, but also about the ever-growing role of the newest mass medium, the Internet, in our culture as a whole.

It is important to remember that "virtual ethnography" is not so much a method in itself, but is often a way of applying in a new context the various methods you have studied in other chapters in this book. It is possible to use observations, interviews, life histories, and so forth in the form of structured chat-room experiences. You may be surprised at how much electronic communication parallels "natural" communication, although you will probably also learn how different it can be. Bird, for example, carried out a remarkably intimate ethnography of a group without ever seeing a human face or hearing a human voice, a strange experience for an anthropologist.

VIRTUAL ETHNOGRAPHY AS A RESEARCH TOOL: A BRIEF OVERVIEW AND HISTORY

Bird's research is one study among many that has found electronic communication to be an exciting new way to understand contemporary culture. Her purpose was to add another dimension to her previous studies of media use, although she found herself becoming interested in the development of this e-mail group as a "community."

The concept of community has long interested anthropologists, who have often been especially concerned with communities having a geographic base—the villages or territories of the traditional peoples who were the focus of anthropological research until relatively recently. At the same time, anthropologists have always found it productive to study associations that are not strictly place-bound, such as societies and organizations that unite people with common interests, even in small societies. As more anthropologists study complex societies and become involved in the multi-disciplinary concerns of globalization, we find that people's associations are increasingly varied, and may not be place-bound. Our social networks include families that may be widely dispersed or involve people who share hobbies, employment, religion, or any number of common experiences.

Non-place communities develop norms and institutional memories based on common experiences, such as the "community" of physicians or Baptists. Virtual communities are essentially an extension of this principle, the main difference being that they develop around computer-mediated communication and that social interactions take place on-line. The focus of much research in this area tends to have been an examination of the difference made by this new communication format: How are virtual and "natural" communities similar and how are they different? We know, for instance, that the existence of the technology can actually make a specialized community possible. While some fans of *Dr. Quinn* might have corresponded or shared their enthusiasm through more conventional means, Bird's research suggested that such a deep commitment would not have been possible without electronic communication. Indeed, many respondents told her that their fandom was a purely private, internal feeling until they discovered other fans through the Internet. Many researchers have thus taken community formation as a central question to be asked through virtual ethnography: What *is* a virtual community, how does electronic communication make new kinds of community possible, and how does it facilitate existing ones? A brief review of some of these studies points to questions you might want to consider in beginning a research project of your own.

One assumes that national identity is already one type of community, but in the "real world," it may be hard to maintain once people become geographically dispersed. How might the Internet affect that process? Daniel Miller and Don Slater found that in Trinidad, for example, the Internet has become the most popular medium for national community maintenance. Nearly the entire population of Trinidad has Internet access and uses it primarily to keep in contact with other "Trinis" from around the world. The two researchers were participant observers of both the "real" and the "virtual" Trinidad, carrying out an ethnography of e-mail discussion lists and contextualizing their data with archival research. They saw "virtual Trini" communities as a method of cultural maintenance and a chance to "lime," a popular Trinidadian pastime roughly equivalent to "hanging out" in the United States. The Trinis were able to reassert and publicly practice their Trinidadian identities, even in the absence of substantial place-bound communities outside the home country. Other researchers have shown how even people who no longer have a significant geographical home (e.g., the Assyrians) have been able to use the Internet to create a sense of identity among a widely scattered population. The Internet is increasingly being used around the world by indigenous groups to maintain identity, argue for their rights, and get the word out to people in their own and other nations.

Other virtual communities are formed on the basis of common interest, such as BlueSky, a MUD (multi-user domain) made up primarily of computer programmers and systems administrators and used nearly exclusively during business hours as a diversion and information source. This on-line community shares characteristics with off-line communities, insofar as its members share various attitudes and behavior patterns. But in this case, computer communication is the very reason for the community to be in existence. BlueSky members are predominantly male, middle-class, technically literate professionals and students. The members avoid anonymity and are overtly hostile to those who try to practice anonymity and identity manipulation. Studies of other on-line interest communities show that, like off-line communities, each one has its own norms about communication, personal identity, gender participation, and so on.

In addition to community formation, education has been a topic of great interest to ethnographers. They have traditionally evaluated programs ethnographically by studying the culture of schools. On-line communication opens up new possibilities for ethnography, just as it is transforming education itself. For example, the Pueblo program is housed in Arizona's elementary schools, where it has become the basis of linkages among students in the United States and in other countries. For the students involved in the creation of Pueblo, the virtual world has, in fact, become a real place.

Some researchers have pointed out that e-communication often mirrors natural communication in such areas as gender styles; predominantly female groups tend to favor a collaborative, nurturing style, while those that are mostly male tend to be confrontational and argumentative. At the same time, the virtual environment allows participants to play with gender identity, as well as with other aspects of identity, such as ethnicity, age, and sexual orientation. Researchers are trying to find out how communication is changed when we know so little about the person with whom we are communicating. More broadly, they are asking whether people's own senses of identity are likely to change in situations where they can become anyone they choose.

Researchers have used analytical techniques such as social-network analysis to look at the interconnections between groups of users and the information flow inherent in an electronic environment. For instance, it is possible to study the intricacies of information flow through the popular game "seven degrees of separation" in which an actor or other public figure is chosen and a series of links between that person and another public figure (or even oneself) are mapped, showing the unlikely connections in a society based on social networks. This game was played long before the advent of electronic communication, but studying it virtually allows us to understand the importance of access to technology and the social networks opened up by that technology.

Life on-line is becoming simply another part of life in the twenty-first century. On-line communities may replicate many of the features of other non-place-based communities, but they also make available new possibilities and new kinds of connections. There are exciting possibilities for on-line ethnographies; indeed, the challenge for the student ethnographer is to decide where to start.

CONDUCTING A VIRTUAL ETHNOGRAPHY: THE PROCESS

The Internet is a virtual world, with any number of potential points of entry, and any number of questions that might be interesting to explore. Before you begin, you need to think carefully about what you're interested in and why it would make sense to study it electronically. It is important to think about one question in particular: Are you interested in studying a phenomenon about which people communicate on the Internet or are you interested in studying the nature of electronic communication itself? These concerns are, of course, related, and they may in fact come together in the course of an extended research project, but they do require different approaches, at least at the outset. For example, Bird once worked with a student who was a recovering alcoholic and who had rejected the spiritual dimensions of Alcoholics Anonymous. He still needed support from other recovering alcoholics and found that some like-minded people had created e-mail groups to share their concerns. While participating as a member, the student used a discussion group to locate people from around the country, whom he then interviewed through e-mail. His main concern was to understand why some people rejected the AA approach, and he elicited a range of opinions, producing an interesting paper as a result. Along the way, he touched upon the emerging role of electronic communication in creating a virtual community, although that aspect of the matter had not been his focus.

On the other hand, another student was interested in how and when a sense of community arises on the Internet. She participated in two e-mail groups; one was largely informational, concerned with issues of relevance to librarians. The other was a support group for mothers of children with disabilities. She found that while the first was active and lively, it was primarily an exchange of objective information and did not encourage the sharing of personal data. In fact, if people became interested in getting to know each other personally, they would move "off-list" to "talk" privately. On the other list, the prime purpose was to create a nurturing community, and the discussion was deeply personal. Participants worked hard to create a sense of community and explicitly referred to the group as a community. The student examined the communication strategies, such as rule-setting, that each group used; her focus was not on what she could learn about librarians or mothers of disabled children, but on how each group used electronic communication to achieve its particular aims.

For a paper in a course on media anthropology, Barber looked more generally at patterns and perceptions of Internet usage in an on-line group. She used both survey research and participant observation, and after familiarizing herself with the group's rules of conduct, she posted a message describing her project and asking for volunteers. Participants were asked questions to determine their level of Internet use, based on hours on-line, number of sites visited, and their perception of themselves on a scale of low to high involvement. She discovered that users with approximately equal numbers of sites visited and total on-line time often rated their use differently. A self-described moderate user might actually spend far more time on-line than someone who self-identified as a heavy user. Barber's research therefore focused on developing norms of Internet usage, rather than on the nature of Internet communication as such.

As anthropologists, our first responsibility in conducting research is to be fair and honest with the people we study; we must never lie to them, invade their privacy, or betray their trust. We should not lose sight of these basic ethical principles even when we are conducting research among people we never see. We should be very skeptical of the suggestion that because the Internet is a public place, the norms of privacy do not apply. A simple content analysis of a public website is not ethically problematic, and it is probably acceptable to quote messages posted on public message boards. But in the latter case, it is probably *not* appropriate to attribute those quotes even to an on-line pseudonym. When studying on-line communities with defined memberships where people are addressing their comments to a particular audience, researchers owe the participants the same courtesy as those they study in the natural world. That is, the members should be informed of your presence, of your intentions, and of your resolve to avoid using real names, e-mail addresses, or other information that could identify them. Since most such groups have formal rules and expectations of behavior, the researcher would be well advised to read and follow them. One researcher, for example, studied a breast-cancer support group whose members were interested in being active participants in her research. By offering drafts of her work for comment and requesting permission to use quotations, her interest in the group was legitimized for the members. She had followed their established procedures of open sharing and acknowledged their right to determine the way in which their comments were used. Bird used the same approach in her research and found that presenting herself in this manner actually opened up interesting possibilities for true collaboration with the respondents.

We must always keep in mind that electronic communication is stripped of all but the written word. Electronic attempts to represent gestures, facial expressions, and tone of voice are crude at best and are easily misinterpreted.

Moreover, the gender, age, and ethnicity of a person to whom we are "talking" can easily be concealed from us. Imagine having developed a detailed life history of a fascinating old man who tells a gripping narrative of growing up on an Indian reservation, only to find out that "he" is actually a twenty-five year old White woman with a vivid imagination and a library of books on Native life. Learn to be critical, to evaluate virtual sources carefully, and avoid making claims of certainty that cannot be backed up by your methodology.

YOUR PROJECT

Choose from among the following suggestions to develop an on-line research project of your own.

- *How does electronic communication help create a sense of ethnic or national identity?* Choose a group in which you are interested. Locate websites, e-mail discussion groups, usenet groups, so on. You might simply observe, perhaps doing a content analysis of an ethnic website to find out, for instance, how Irish or Cree identity is defined on the Web. Who created the site? What kind of image is the site attempting to create? Does it incorporate a guestbook or other opportunity for feedback? How does such a mechanism contribute to the mutual development of ethnic identity? Is ethnic pride dependent on demonizing or denigrating other ethnic groups, and if so, how is this goal accomplished? On the other hand, you might prefer to participate as well as observe. Lurk on an e-mail list or usenet group and look for ways people discuss ethnic identity. Then join in, although you should avoid disrupting the group with your own research agenda. Conduct interviews with selected members.

- *What is the nature of virtual communities?* Do your own study of any kind of on-line community—a professional or interest group, an extended family listserv, a support group. The possibilities are endless. Think about the questions discussed above: How are rules of conduct made and applied, and how is order maintained? What are the norms of anonymity? Do members extend their relationship outside the virtual environment? How significant is the community in people's lives? You might focus on particular techniques: participant observation might be the best way to look at rules and community-building strategies, while interviews might be more effective in finding out how members feel about the community.

- *What impact is the time spent on-line having on society?* If a person spends six hours a day at her computer, what does this activity replace? Would she be reading, writing letters, socializing in person? What happens to couples and families when individuals spend a great deal of time on-line? Can on-line interaction actually transform a shy person into a more sociable individual? There are many ways to approach these questions, and you should refer to other chapters in this book for ideas. For example, you could conduct on-line life histories, asking people to write or talk about their lives in detail, with special emphasis in this case on how the computer may have changed their lives. Or you might use on-line diaries, in which people are asked to record their thoughts at particular times of day. Your focus might be the family, a couple, or even one individual, producing a detailed, intimate portrait of that person's interaction with technology.

- *How is differential access affecting our society?* Internet technology is touching the lives not only of dedicated users, but also of those with limited or even no access to the on-line world. You might explore the impact of the so-called "digital divide" that separates those with easy access from those without. Do teenagers who can only access the Internet for thirty minutes a day in a school media center use it differently from those with access in their own rooms at home? What are the educational impacts of easy access? How is fluent computer and Internet literacy related to questions of social class or status? Such questions might best be explored through a combination of virtual and natural ethnography—for example, interviewing on-line combined with observing behavior at home.

- *What impact is the Internet having on education?* How does using the Internet as a teaching medium change the interaction between students and teachers? How do on-line student discussion groups contribute to learning? It is very likely that you will have at least some of your own educational experiences on-line; use this opportunity to develop your ethnographic skills while thinking more deeply about your own learning processes.

- *How does the technology affect the very nature of communication?* In this case, the emphasis is not so much on the content of people's communication, but on the act of communication itself. When we don't know who people are, we can take on many identities. We can certainly present ourselves differently in different "real" social situations, of course (a process sometimes referred to as "style shifting"); but how does this process change when the medium itself allows us to communicate as if we were of a different racial category or a different gender? Does the fact that we cannot see faces or respond to body language affect the nature of language and communication?

Whichever project you select, please make sure that your final report contains not only information about what you found out about the particular topic, but also some of your personal reflections on the process of doing ethnography on-line.

A FEW SELECTED READINGS FOR FURTHER INFORMATION

Bird, S. Elizabeth. 1996. Not My Fantasy: The Persistence of Indian Imagery in *Dr. Quinn: Medicine Woman*. In *Dressing in Feathers: The Construction of the Indian in American Popular Culture*, ed. S. Elizabeth Bird, 245–262. Boulder, CO: Westview.

———. 1999. Chatting on Cynthia's Porch: Creating Community in an E-mail Fan Group. *Southern Communication Journal* 65(1):49–65.

Gabrial, Albert. 1998. Assyrians: "3,000 Years of History, Yet the Internet Is Our Only Home." *Cultural Survival Quarterly* 21(4):42–44.

Hine, Christine. 2000. *Virtual Ethnography*. London: Sage.

Jones, Steven G., ed. 1998. *Cybersociety 2.0*. London: Sage.

———. 1999. *Doing Internet Research: Critical Issues and Methods for Examining the Net*. London: Sage.

Markham, Annette. 1996. *Life On-Line: Researching Real Experience in Virtual Space*. New York: AltaMira.

Miller, Daniel, and Don Slater. 2000. *The Internet: An Ethnographic Approach*. New York: Berg.

Nardi, Bonnie, and Vicki O'Day. 1999. *Information Ecologies: Using Technology with Heart*. Cambridge, MA: MIT Press.

14

Developing an
Electronic Ethnography

Alvin W. Wolfe & Guy Hagen

A RESEARCH PROJECT

Ethnographic observations by practicing anthropologists studying the operations of health and human service agencies in the Tampa Bay area revealed a common need by these agencies for useable, readily accessible information to support the functions of planning, monitoring, evaluation, management, and budgeting. Individual agencies typically gather as much information as possible given the limitations of their own resources of personnel, time, and money. The results are often disappointing, and the process is very inefficient. Both the ethnographers and the agency staff were hard-pressed to learn who is doing what for whom with what resources and with what effect. To address this common problem, Mary Rust, a planner with the city of Tampa who had earned an M.A. in anthropology at the University of South Florida, approached Alvin Wolfe, one of her former professors, with a proposal to develop a Human Services Information System (HSIS). Rust,

Wolfe, and several students convened a planning workshop attended by representatives of more than twenty-five agencies. The workshop participants agreed on a number of points: that the need for information is vital to their ability to carry out their duties; that they intended to meet that need; that the system should ultimately serve the widest feasible range of functions; that its organization should have the form of a consortium of agencies.

It is difficult for an entire human services system to organize for collective action. The system of services for children and families in the Tampa Bay metropolitan area, for example, consists of more than a thousand firms or official agencies and several thousand less formal programs providing hundreds of types of services to hundreds of thousands of persons. Each political unit (city, county, state) wants to keep control over its own agencies and programs, so political forces inhibit the expenditure of public funds for cooperative endeavors that crosscut these boundaries. Moreover, there is little profit in the provision of human services, so the system is not structured by market principles of supply and demand. As a result, the human-services system is almost unmanageable because of the complexity of the system itself. Its overall structure resembles a network rather than a hierarchical bureaucratic organization, even though it is composed of hierarchically structured subsets. Even as a network, it is not beautifully symmetrical like the web of a healthy spider, but asymmetrical, with dense clusters and gaping holes—the infamous "holes in the safety net," or the equally infamous "cracks through which clients fall." Nonetheless, there is some kind of whole in operation, and that whole can be grasped by using the electronic and network analytic tools made available to us by engineering and mathematics.

Because human beings stand behind all the entities in these complex systems, we as anthropologists realized that the people involved in them connect organizations to one another; the people themselves are in turn connected to one another by their common involvement in the organizations. In developing the HSIS, we were able to employ mathematical techniques to help us make sense of these heretofore bewildering networks, a process we call electronic ethnography. Just as earlier ethnographers learned to use mapping instruments, still cameras, audio recorders, movie cameras, and video equipment, so modern electronic ethnographers must learn to use current technology and the mathematical analysis that supports it. The social-network analysis that produced the HSIS took advantage of computers to augment traditional ethnographic techniques, allowing for the analysis of larger communities and more complex structures than would be possible using traditional manual techniques. Computer analysis also enabled us to probe the nature of an "electronic community" whose members are not defined by common physical location, but rather by common interest (in this case, the provision of human services in a large urban area). The HSIS is a device for mapping how communication takes place across this dispersed (and, on the surface, chaotic) community whose members deal with each other through e-mail and other electronic media, rather than in face-to-face interactions. The

HSIS was first presented in a paper by Wolfe, Rust, and Patricia Sorrells delivered at the annual meeting of the Society for Applied Anthropology in 1980.

ELECTRONIC ETHNOGRAPHY AND NETWORK ANALYSIS AS TOOLS OF ETHNOGRAPHIC RESEARCH

Traditional ethnographers described cultures that were expressed through communications between a few thousand persons. For example, Raymond Firth's classic study was conducted on Tikopia, a Pacific island with a population of 1,300 in 1929; even if everyone on the island communicated with everyone else, the total number of relationships would only have been about 845,000. By contrast, ethnographers who work in modern societies confront numbers of a vastly greater magnitude. The population of the U.S. alone is 280,000,000 according to the 2000 census. Moreover, modern communications media make it possible for these vast numbers of people to share information instantaneously. Even as long ago as 1980, 150,000,000 people worldwide saw and simultaneously experienced the Super Bowl. In that same era, half the households in the U.S.—almost 100,000,000 persons, watched the television miniseries *Roots*. The scale and scope of communication has increased greatly in the ensuing two decades. In this milieu, old-fashioned ethnography cannot do a complete job.

Technology has enabled unprecedented new levels of communication and interaction among human populations. New communities, cultural norms, and elements of language have been facilitated by the growth of the Internet. Complex interest groups ("chat" and "news" groups) form around shared interests, and dense webs of electronic communication enable long-distance interactions in ways never even imagined until very recently. Web pages are electronic representations of companies, communities, and individuals. There are an estimated 800 million web pages today, with approximately one million pages being added every day. Broadcast and broadband media enable the near-simultaneous interaction of millions of people. All these developments make up a world that ethnographers must cope with. Social scientists are just beginning to adapt methodologies to explore this electronic frontier, and ethnographic analysis must keep pace.

Since the beginning of ethnographic fieldwork, the preparation, collation, indexing, and storing of field notes has been among the most important of activities for researchers, for only if such details are carefully attended to can the relevant information be retrieved when needed. Surely it was such tasks as organizing the information derived from observations of hitherto unknown cultures that led anthropologists to conceptualize culture as a complex whole, divisible into various domains and levels, yet integrated through relations among those domains and levels. As anthropologists took into account more of the internal variability within traditional cultures that used to be stereotyped as "simple," their informal methods of handling data were strained. The matter was complicated when they began dealing with the differentiation and specialization of modern societies. For a long period in the middle of the twentieth century, the major statements about complex societies were derived from the macro-level data sets of economists, political scientists, and sociologists, while anthropologists and other ethnographers tended to provide only "local color." We believe that ethnographers can and should do more.

It may yet be within our capabilities to do holistic ethnographies of complex systems analogous to what used to be done in traditional cultures. We assume that culture must be described not only in terms of the locally accepted standards, but also with respect to variances from those standards. It will come as no surprise that the amount of data necessary to record not only the norms but the variations as well is massive. Nevertheless, we should not be dismayed or discouraged. Technological advances have enabled new data-processing tools that can be used to surmount these challenges, including the introduction of new levels of computing capacity. Today's microprocessors are approximately 100,000 times faster than the earliest processors. Industry experts predict that computing power will continue to double every eighteen months. Within twenty years, individual computers may be more powerful than all the combined computing power currently available in Silicon Valley. Moreover, data storage becomes more efficient because of increased capacity of each unit as well as distribution among units.

In addition to rapidly and efficiently handling masses of data, computer programs can now model the complex relations among data domains and levels. Database-management systems incorporate methods for handling large sets of data that are logically organized to satisfy a variety of users' requirements. Instead of relying on sequentially organized records whose relations derive basically from the fact that they draw certain attribute values from common domains, modern databases can be hierarchical or relational in organization. If they are hierarchical, they originate in a root and the records branch out in one-to-many relations, toward terminal records, as segmentary lineage systems or bureaucracies do in social life. On the other hand, record structures may have a network form, wherein each record may be related directly to several other records—a very complicated architecture that, alas, models the complexity of most sociocultural phenomena.

To illustrate how the data of a reasonably complex system can be organized, we can take a look at the schema for the HSIS (see Figure 1). Each box represents a table (or record type); for example, the "firm" record has information about an agency. The lines represent direct hierarchical linkages creating a set of tables, one table relating to others in one-to-many relations. Many-to-many relations, on the other hand, occur when one firm operates programs at several sites and one site houses operations of several facilities.

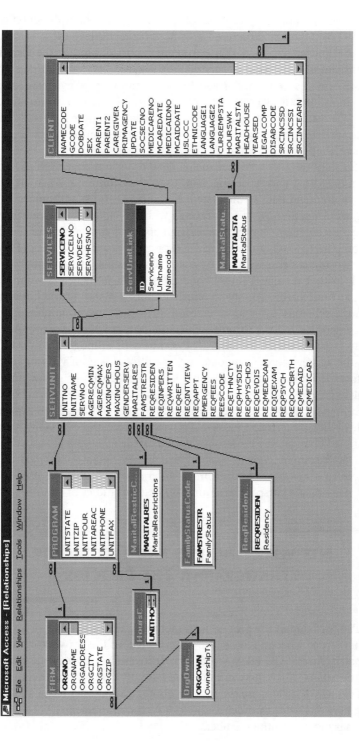

Figure 1   Types of Records (Tables) Related in HSIS Database

The database permits easy retrieval of information in either direction on the network. From data so structured, it is possible to retrieve the specific information desired and to have that particular report printed in the format desired. Instead of some kind of generalizing statistical statement that so many thousand services were performed by some number of agencies, one can make a more descriptive statement closer to the reality of the situation, preserving the variation among agencies or firms, programs, clients, and so forth, as well as preserving information about their relationships. An excerpt from such a report is shown in Table 1.

It is important to note that such a database is not conceived as fixed. In addition to storing and retrieving data, users may continuously insert, delete, update, and amend data as the system that is being modeled changes. We are dealing with a system open to exchange with the environment and therefore offering management capabilities beyond its own narrow limits. Feedback from component to component provides for maintenance of levels of flow and for making adjustments within the system. There is also the potential for feed-forward, in that predicted future conditions might influence the state of the system, an anticipatory quality obviously useful for planning and forecasting.

Such schemas can model cultural structure, and computer programs can provide the windows through which an ethnographer of a complex society may view different domains. The richness of ethnographic detail transcends the aggregation of raw data, our traditional way of viewing information storage. Rather, such a system offers the capability of looking back through aggregate information over the course of time while viewing complex relationships on multi-level plans at the same point in time. Such capabilities offer flexibility for decision makers. Patterns emerge and overviews are feasible; planned change may be designed based on the small picture as well as the large. Database-management systems that were originally designed to meet the needs of business and government enterprises can now be used to help achieve the holistic perspective of anthropological studies of culture.

NETWORK ANALYSIS AND ELECTRONIC ETHNOGRAPHY: THE PROCESS

The first step in the process is to identify a personal network by preparing a new spreadsheet document in order to record the network under study in a matrix format. In other words, the software helps to create a table in which members of the network are listed simultaneously as row labels and column labels. Matrices are the most common format for storing and manipulating network data. In order to find out who communicates with whom, it is necessary to survey the members.

Table 1 Report produced by the Human Services Information System

Department of Anthropology, University of South Florida, Tampa, Florida 33620

Program: Agency for Community Treatment Services HSIS
   Database No: 12100
   4211 E Busch Blvd
   Tampa, FL 33617-5916
   813 9886096
   Type and Funding: Non-profit, Incorporated
   (Voluntary) FEES

Program: ACTS, Adult Residential Detox
   6806 N Nebraska Ave
   Tampa, FL 33604
   813 2389505
   Program Services: alcohol counseling services
   detox serv for drug abuse
   residential trtmnt alcoholism

Program: ACTS, Agcy for Comm Trtmt Svcs
   4211 E Busch Blvd
   Tampa, FL 33617-5916
   813 9883533
   Program Services: alcohol abuse educa/info serv
   alcohol counseling services
   drug counseling services

Program: Adolescent Group Home, ACTS
   3806 W M.L.King Blvd.
   Tampa, FL 33614
   813 8700578
   Program Services: residential trtmnt alcoholism
   residential trtmnt drug dpndn-

Program: Adolescent Receiving, ACTS
   8620 N Dixon Ave
   Tampa, FL 33604
   813 9314669
   Program Services: alcohol counseling services
   detox serv for alcoholics
   detox serv for drug abuse
   drug counseling services

Program: Agency for Community Treatment Services, ACTS
   4612 N 56th St
   Tampa, FL 33610
   813 2464899
   Program Services: juvenile counselling
   psychological assessment
   psychological therapy

Program: Alcohol Community Treatment
   4403 W M.L.King Blvd
   Tampa, FL 33614-7604
   813 8791649
   Program Services: alcohol counseling services
   internships
   residential trmnt alcoholism
   transitional serv-alcoholism

Program: Dependency Group Home, ACTS
   3812 W M.L. King Blvd.
   Tampa, FL 33614
   813 8702236
   Program Services:
   foster care – dependency
   group home – pre-dlnquent youth

Program: Halfway House ACTS
   4403 W M.L.King Blvd
   Tampa, FL 33614
   813 8759645
   Program Services:
   internships

Program: HARP, Residential Svcs, ACTS
   8702 Stark Road
   Seffner, FL 33584
   813 6216051
   Program Services:
   resid.care,long term,mental r-

Program: Homeless Day Center, ACTS
   6220 N Nebraska Ave
   Tampa, FL 33604
   813 2376630
   Program Services:
   shltr-newcmrs,travlrs,homeless

Program: Outpatient Counseling ACTS
   1815 W Sligh Ave
   Tampa, FL 33604 -5811
   813 2376630
   Program Services:
   alcohol abuse educa/info serv
   alcohol counseling services
   drug counseling services

Program: Outpatient Counseling, ACTS
   4211 E Busch Blvd
   Tampa, FL 33617-5916
   813 9883533
   Program Services:
   alcohol counseling services
   drug counseling services

Program: Pinellas Domiciliary
   3575 Old Keystone Road
   Tarpon Springs, FL 34689
   813 4612881
   Program Services:
   alcohol counseling services
   internships
   residential trtmnt alcoholism
   transitional serv-alcoholism

Program: Youth Outpatient, ACTS
   8620 N Dixon Ave
   Tampa, FL 33604
   813 9314669
   Program Services:
   alcohol counseling services
   drug counseling services

Program: Youth Overlay Services, ACTS
   3806 W M.L.King Blvd.
   Tampa, FL 33614
   813 8700578
   Program Services:
   alcohol counseling services
   drug abuse ed/info serv
   drug counseling services

The number of individuals in a network is its size (represented by n). People will have differently sized networks depending on how socially active, influential, or popular they are. In addition to size, a network may be characterized by its density, which is the proportion of active links in a network to the maximum possible links. Another characteristic of a network is its prestige factor. Not all connections in the matrix will be reciprocal. Sometimes one person lists another as a contact, but the latter does not necessarily list the former. Individuals who are cited more frequently than others are said to have prestige. In the HSIS, for example, individuals with high prestige were the ones most likely to have access to important information required across the network.

YOUR PROJECT

This project entails the construction of a simple network database. You will explore an "ego network" of connections within a small group of individuals and will use simple network-analysis techniques to identify social and qualitative characteristics of that group and its members. The requirements for this project are limited to tools that should be available to most students: a computer with a spreadsheet program (e.g., Microsoft Excel, Lotus, Appleworks) and an e-mail account. More ambitious students might want to explore the UCINET5 network-analysis software that is available at http://www.analytictech.com. Depending on your personal interests, we present two options for your project. If you are primarily interested in augmenting traditional ethnographic techniques, you may explore your own personal network of friends and family. If you are interested in exploring the electronic medium, you may collect data on e-mail communication among your friends.

As noted above, the first step is to prepare a spreadsheet. Make a list of the people you communicate with most frequently (between ten and twenty individuals) and enter them into the database. If you are exploring an e-mail network, work from your e-mail program's contact list. Imagine that your network includes you, your professor, and nine friends. The resulting matrix might look something like Table 2.

Any cell that contains a "1" indicates that a network connection exists between individuals whose rows and columns intersect; "0" indicates a lack of connection. For purposes of this example, a network connection signifies that frequent communication (e-mail or otherwise) exists between members. Since we need not be concerned with people who send e-mail to themselves, put a 0 in cells where the row and column labels are the same.

Next, contact each individual in the network. Provide each member with a copy of your list and ask each of them to indicate every individual that they have regular communication with (or each individual who is on their e-mail contact list). The resulting filled-in matrix might look something like Table 3.

Table 2 Sample Network Matrix

	you@university.edu	prof@university.edu	friend1@apple.com	friend2@msn.com	friend3@yahoo.com	friend4@hotmail.com	friend5@cs.com	friend6@aol.com	friend7@networks.net	friend8@insna.org	friend9@whitehouse.gov
you@university.edu	0	1	1	1	1	1	1	1	1	1	1
prof@university.edu											
friend1@apple.com											
friend2@msn.com											
friend3@yahoo.com											
friend4@hotmail.com											
friend5@cs.com											
friend6@aol.com											
friend7@networks.net											
friend8@insna.org											
friend9@whitehouse.gov											

Table 3 Complete "Ego Network" Matrix for Ego and Ten Contacts

	you@university.edu	prof@university.edu	friend1@apple.com	friend2@msn.com	friend3@yahoo.com	friend4@hotmail.com	friend5@cs.com	friend6@aol.com	friend7@networks.net	friend8@insna.org	friend9@whitehouse.gov
you@university.edu	0	1	1	1	1	1	1	1	1	1	1
prof@university.edu	1	0	1	1	0	0	0	1	1	0	1
friend1@apple.com	1	0	0	0	1	1	0	0	0	1	1
friend2@msn.com	0	1	1	0	1	1	1	1	0	0	1
friend3@yahoo.com	1	0	1	1	0	0	0	0	0	1	0
friend4@hotmail.com	1	1	0	1	1	0	1	0	0	1	1
friend5@cs.com	1	0	1	0	0	1	0	1	0	1	1
friend6@aol.com	0	1	1	0	1	0	0	0	1	0	1
friend7@networks.net	1	0	0	1	0	0	0	0	0	1	0
friend8@insna.org	1	0	0	1	0	1	0	0	0	0	1
friend9@whitehouse.gov	0	0	1	0	0	0	0	0	0	1	0

You can now calculate the density of your network by using the spreadsheet's *sum* function. First add the total number of links in each column and then add up the total of these values. The result will be the number of links in the network. Divide this number by the maximum possible links (calculated with the formula [n × (n − 1)]. Results can range from 0 (lowest density) to 1 (highest density). How might you explain the density pattern that characterizes your network?

Your first calculation in the density analysis—the total number of links per column—is also your measure of prestige. The individual with the highest score is the one with the most prestige. How might you explain the patterns of prestige that you find in your network?

You may conclude your analysis by constructing a sociogram, a visual graph of the network that will help you clarify its characteristics. Sociograms representing very large networks such as the HSIS will, of course, be extremely complex. But for the purposes of this project, there is a relatively simple method: start by placing labels for the individuals in your network around a circle. Draw a line between each pair of labels that are connected (i.e., represented by a "1" in a cell at either the row–column intersection or the column–row intersection, which may be different, depending on the prestige factor). Here is a simple sociogram based on our example:

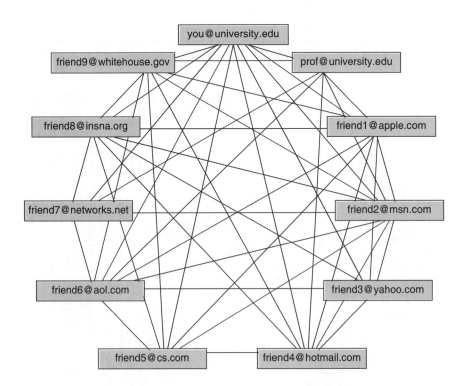

Draw a sociogram for your own network. Does the graph suggest anything interesting? Are the density and prestige calculations revealed?

A FEW SELECTED READINGS FOR FURTHER INFORMATION

Chakrabarti, S., B. Dom, S. Ravi Kumar, P. Raghavan, S. Rajagopalan, and A. Tompkins. 1999. Hypersearching the Web. *Scientific American* June:54–60.

Garton, Laura, Caroline Haythornthwaite, and Barry Wellman. 1997. Studying Online Social Networks. *Journal of Computer Mediated Communication* 3(1):1–10.

15

Composing
Autoethnographic Stories

Leigh Berger & Carolyn Ellis

The students in my "Writing Lives" class stare at me expectantly. We are about to discuss Carolyn Ellis's *Final Negotiations: A Story of Love, Loss, and Chronic Illness.* The book details the loss of her partner, Gene Weinstein, and also describes her approach to writing. I open today's conversation by throwing out a question: "What was the purpose of this book?" I am met by a full minute of silence.

"Well, Professor Berger," Dan, one of my more talkative students, ventures, "I think that Ellis wanted to make sense of the death of her partner, Gene."

I nod while replying, "Okay, good. Any other feelings about the purpose of this book?"

Carrie raises her hand and says, "It seems like it was partially to make sense of his death, but she also interpreted what happened from a social science perspective and used what other social scientists had to say."

I smile. "Great point. But why would she want to connect social science to the death of her partner?" Another few moments of silence. This time, there doesn't seem to be anyone with the courage to try a response, so I ask a follow-up question: "What is Carolyn Ellis's job?"

"Social scientist!" several students respond simultaneously.

"What do social scientists do?" I ask.

"Study people and society," Dan replies, running a hand through his closely cropped, dark hair.

"How?" I inquire.

"They observe things," Jennifer, another student, explains as she leans forward. "You know, some go hang out with people for a while and take notes on what goes on."

"That's called ethnography," I interrupt her, writing the word on the board. "But if ethnography usually involves studying other people, what is Ellis doing?"

"Some sort of combination of ethnography and autobiography," Erin, one of my quieter students, pipes up.

"Excellent," I encourage her. "Exactly! And that is called autoethnography." I write this word on the board below "ethnography." "Carolyn Ellis is using her own experience as a starting point for studying how death and chronic illness are experienced, and she is writing in a more literary way to draw readers into those events." I am cut off by a hand going up in the back of the room. "Yes, Chad?"

"But why is that not just a memoir or something—I mean, how does her experience get classified as social science?"

"Good question. Would you say that death and illness are important to our society? Are they events commonly experienced by people?"

There is agreement as students nod and murmur, "Yes."

"Well, couldn't Ellis have gone out and conducted a statistical survey about how people deal with death and loss instead of using an autoethnographic method?" A few students nod while others shake their heads "no." To clarify, I ask, "Why didn't she do that?"

"Well, getting statistics is fine, but I don't think that was her goal," Carrie says thoughtfully. "I mean, statistics give important information about how many people experience something, but wasn't Ellis's purpose to have readers feel what she was feeling?"

"Or feel their own losses," Dan throws in.

I reply, "Well, if we accept that as one of her goals, let me ask if, while reading this book, you connected to her story."

"Yes," Dan says. "It made me think about my grandfather's death, actually. Even though he had cancer, not emphysema, there were still a lot of similarities. Because my grandfather was sick for so long, I remember that I felt relieved when I knew it was almost over, but then that made me feel guilty— like Ellis describes. Reading this also made me realize a lot of the things my grandmother must have gone through because she took care of him."

Carrie's green eyes mist over with tears as she says, "Ellis really described a lot of the feelings I had when my mother died. My mother had diabetes for most of her life, and little by little she began losing control of different functions. Ellis was really good at describing how your feelings go back and forth between wanting the person to finally be in peace, but not wanting to lose them."

"For those of you who were reminded of your own losses, did the book also give you new ways of thinking about or dealing with those deaths?"

"Definitely," says Carrie. "It made me understand that other people also felt what I did. Like I wasn't alone, and it helped me feel less guilty about the times I wanted my mother's life to finally end."

Erin added, "I haven't experienced loss of a loved one yet, but I'm still glad I read this work. I think I'll be better prepared now when I do."

The class is quiet and contemplative for a few seconds. Finally I say, "What I'm hearing is that this story provided a window into loss that resonates with your own knowledge about how the world works and helps you anticipate future experience. And it also opened new possibilities for understanding illness and death. Do you agree with that assessment, Chad?"

Chad nods and says, "Yeah, but . . . I'm still wondering. How can this be scientifically valid?"

"The goals of autoethnography are not validity—or accuracy—in the traditional sense of the word. Instead, autoethnographers attempt to communicate emotional truth." I try to think of a way to explain this clearly. "In autoethnography, it is the job of readers to determine if they think the story is honest and if it rings true to their experiences. The whole idea of an autoethnography is to show readers ways they are similar to and different from others in the world. If Carolyn Ellis's book moves us to consider the experience of loss, if it makes us question the ways we can relate to her story, and the ways we might not, then we are learning about the social world. And," I add, "don't forget that Ellis is trained as a social scientist. She looks at the world through the lens of that expertise. So even when using her own experiences, she is analyzing and drawing conclusions as a social scientist and giving readers insights into social processes."

"But I'd still want to know if her experiences are generalizable," Chad says. "That's what we learned to ask in my methods class. I mean, it was just her experience. She didn't select a sample or anything, or even talk to other people about their experiences for comparison."

"I think her work *is* generalizable," Carrie replies thoughtfully. "But she's thinking of generalizability in a different way from most social scientists. She's not thinking of it from a sampling point of view, but from an audience perspective. I mean, you can see from our responses to her story that we've experienced some of what she did."

"I think she'd say our experience resonated with hers," says Erin, brushing some of her red hair behind one shoulder.

"And remember, her goal is to evoke experiences from readers, to open up conversations about them, not to accurately represent the mean experience," I remind them, very happy with the conversation we're having. "I think I see that happening today, with Carrie and Dan discussing how Ellis's work reminds them of their experiences with loss. Ellis provides a description of what's possible, not what's typical, and then she asks the audience to compare their experience with hers and with others, talking about how they're similar and different. So in essence you, the reader, become a social scientist, analyzing and drawing comparisons."

"Cool," says Pete, speaking his first words of the semester.

I glance at the clock. "I hate to do this, but we should also discuss the other piece you read for today, which is a paper based on my two-year ethnography of Dalet Shalom, a Messianic Jewish congregation. We can continue to talk about autoethnography as it applies to this paper." As the students shuffle through readings, I ask, "What makes the Messianic movement unique?"

Jim, who hasn't spoken yet today, answers, "They're essentially both Jewish and Christian."

I nod and say, "Yes. They consider themselves Jewish, and observe Jewish holidays and celebrations, but they believe Jesus—Yeshua—is the Messiah."

"Is Yeshua really the Hebrew pronunciation of Jesus?" Jennifer asks.

"Yes," I reply. "So they are a group who lives on the boundary between Jewish and Christian, and this makes them controversial not only within the Jewish community, but also within the mainstream Christian community. How is that for complicated?" The students chuckle in response. "Now, in what ways would you say this is similar to Ellis's work?"

"It's written like a story, too," Carrie explains.

"Yes, good. How else?"

"Well, you talk a lot about your . . ." Erin searches for an appropriate word, "feelings about what's going on and talk about your own experiences as a Jewish person."

I am pleased that Erin is speaking so freely today. "I do. My starting point for understanding Dalet Shalom is my own feelings and reactions. So, what makes this work similar to Ellis's is its use of autoethnography. What makes it different?"

"Ellis's work focuses more clearly on her own story about the loss of Gene. Yours is about you, but its main focus is on a religious congregation." Dan leans back in his chair.

"Yes. Essentially, what's going on in this piece is two parallel journeys. We have my exploration of this Messianic congregation, but at the same time I show how I am also on a quest to examine my own questions of Jewish identity and spiritual experience. Why do you think I chose to use a narrative technique to write about my study?"

Jim raises his hand and says, "Well, it's pretty hard to describe religious experience in an objective way. How would you explain what faith feels like without using a story?"

"Good point, Jim. Think about your own experiences of spirituality, or maybe the experiences of others you know. Religious systems themselves are stories—the Bible, Native American traditions—they're all based on storytelling. Also, Messianic Judaism is evangelical, so the congregation worships in a highly emotional way and most people there express having a personal experience with God. Narrative autoethnography is a style that naturally lends itself to accessing the personal and emotional." I pause. "I think some of you are lost," I say, looking at a few students who furl their eyebrows and look around as if they have no notion of what's going on. "I think we need to step back and really think about what autoethnography is." I glance at the clock. "Unfortunately, we're out of time. How about next time we pick up with a discussion of the history of autoethnography so you can clearly understand these issues." Looks of relief cross many faces. "See you all then. Have a good afternoon!" I call after them as they rush for the door.

I gather my notes and head to my office. On the way, I stop at Carolyn Ellis's office and knock on the door. "Come in," her voice calls. As I enter the room, Carolyn turns around and smiles.

"Do you have a minute?" I ask.

"Sure." After moving some piles of books out of my way, she beckons me to sit in a black recliner next to her desk.

"I just got out of class. We were discussing *Final Negotiations* and one of my papers about Dalet Shalom," I explain.

"Really? Any interesting reactions?"

"A few were able to connect your story to their own experiences of loss. Most of them seemed to understand the purpose of autoethnography, but some were clearly confused. One student wanted to know how this was considered social science. And they asked about validity and generalizability. We ran out of time, but I told them I want to discuss the history of autoethnography next time."

Carolyn looks contemplative as she responds. "You could always give them a written history and description of autoethnography that they can read. In fact, I have something I wrote for my classes." She rises and rummages through one of her file cabinets, pulling out a paper and handing it to me. Looking down, I see "A Brief History of Autoethnography."

"Thank you," I say. "This may be just what I need."

"Then I'd probably give them a list of articles about autoethnography."

"I thought of that already," I respond.

"And maybe a few more autoethnographic stories," Carolyn continues, "and ask them to use these as models for writing their own experiences. You could give them 'There Are Survivors,' where I focus on my own experience. And I just happen to have an outline of steps to follow for writing personal narratives," she adds as she rummages through her file cabinet, producing a yellowed sheet of paper. "Here you go," she says, handing the paper to me.

"And I could give them a piece from my dissertation on the Messianic congregation," I say, "where I wrote about others but included myself as a character. I'll also write an outline of steps to follow for that kind of writing."

"Good idea," Carolyn says, beaming. "The only way they're really going to learn about autoethnography is to write it themselves."

"That certainly was true for me," I respond. Carolyn smiles a knowing smile as I get up to leave.

I immediately read Carolyn's paper on the history of autoethnography and copy it for my students. The next day I hand it out to my class and I review the paper as they read. Here is the paper:

A Brief History of Autoethnography

Autoethnography is an autobiographical style of writing and research that connects personal and cultural experience. Autoethnographers not only observe the world around them, but also examine their internal perceptions and feelings about their place in that world. Usually written in the first-person voice, autoethnographic works can take various forms: poetry, short stories, fiction, novels, photographic essays, and social-science prose. These accounts include characters, action, dialogue, and emotional response. Autoethnographers ideally use all their senses, their bodies, movement, feeling, and their whole being to learn about others.

The term "autoethnography" has been around since the 1970s. Like many terms used by social scientists, the meanings and applications of autoethnography are now so varied that it is hard to provide a precise definition. Autoethnography is linked to the feminist movement and the social-scientific questioning of relationships between researchers and subjects. Many feminist writers advocate making the researcher's presence, values, and biases known in the writing of research and embrace the idea of research based in personal experience. The distanced, "objective" voice of the (usually) white, male researcher no longer seemed to address the issues that were being raised by newer ethnographers who were increasingly members of racial and ethnic minorities, lower-class, and/or citizens of the Third or Fourth World. As a result, many social scientists questioned the ways ethnography had traditionally been carried out and written about.

Autoethnography encourages ethnographers to develop a relationship with those studied, to treat them as co-researchers, to share authority, and to assist participants to author their own lives in their own voices. Readers, too, take a more active role as they are invited into the author's world, asked to respond to and discuss the events being described, and are stimulated to use what they learn to reflect on, understand, and cope with their own lives.

Essentially, autoethnography opens a dialogue among the researcher, participant, and reader. In the sharing and co-creation of stories, the goal of this conversation is for researcher and participants to understand one another better and for readers to interpret and form opinions about what they are reading. Autoethnography invites readers to accompany the author on a journey and to add their own emotions and reactions as they travel into worlds of new discoveries and possibilities.

"That helps, but I'm still having trouble," Chad says after reading about autoethnography. A few students, who haven't been participating, nod in agreement. "Are there other things we could read like this that might help us understand autoethnography better?"

"Well, yes, glad you asked. I just happen to have a short list here for those of you who want to read further." I hand out the list:

Readings on Autoethnography

Berger, Leigh. 1997. Between the Candy Store and the Mall: The Spiritual Loss of a Father. *Journal of Personal and Interpersonal Loss* 2(4):397–409.

Bochner, Arthur P. 1994. Perspectives on Inquiry II: Theories and Stories. In *Handbook of Interpersonal Communication*, 2nd ed., ed. M. Knap and G. R. Miller, 21–41. Newbury Park, CA: Sage.

———. 1997. It's About Time: Narrative and the Divided Self. *Qualitative Inquiry* 3:418–438.

Denzin, Norman K. 1997. *Interpretive Ethnography: Ethnographic Practices for the 21st Century.* Thousand Oaks, CA: Sage.

Ellis, Carolyn. 1995. *Final Negotiations: A Story of Love, Loss, and Chronic Illness.* Philadelphia: Temple University Press.

Ellis, Carolyn, and Arthur P. Bochner, eds. 1996. *Composing Ethnography: Alternative Forms of Qualitative Writing.* Walnut Creek, CA: AltaMira.

———. 2000 Autoethnography, Personal Narrative, Reflexivity: Researcher as Subject. In *Handbook of Qualitative Research*, 2nd ed., ed. Norman Denzin and Yvonna Lincoln, 733–768. Newbury Park, CA: Sage.

Kiesinger, Christine. 1998. From Interview to Story: Writing "Abbie's Life." *Qualitative Inquiry* 4(1):71–95.

Richardson, Laurel. 1994. Writing as a Method of Inquiry. In *Handbook of Qualitative Research*, ed. Norman Denzin and Yvonna Lincoln, 516–529. Thousand Oaks, CA: Sage.

"The reading will help, but I think one of the difficulties you're having in understanding autoethnography is that you haven't experienced writing one yourselves," I say, delighted that I am prepared. "So, I've come up with two possible assignments you can choose from. The first is to write a personal narrative similar to the style of Ellis's *Final Negotiations*. The second is to write about others, but include yourself as a primary character, as I did in my work on Messianic Judaism."

I begin handing out the assignment. "Each assignment begins with a brief story to remind you of the two approaches. The first is an excerpt from a story Carolyn wrote about the death of her brother, Rex. Mine is another piece from my ethnography of Dalet Shalom. Following each story are step-by-step instructions for each assignment. Let's read them over now. Then you can decide which one you want to do."

"There Are Survivors": Telling a Story of Sudden Death
by Carolyn Ellis

Rex was scheduled to arrive in Tampa today, Friday, January 13, 1982. Although I was supposed to meet him at 4:30, his plane was just ready for take-off from Washington when I called the airline at 3:45. Since I had invited several friends to dinner, I was glad for the extra time.

"Hey, what you doing?" my older brother, Art, asks when I pick up the ringing phone. I am surprised to hear from him, and, in spite of the lightness of his words, detect worry in his voice. Rather quickly he asks, "Has Rex gotten there yet?"

"No, his plane has been delayed. Why?" Already I feel alarmed.

"Oh, someone called Mom and said a plane had crashed, and she thought they said something about Tampa. I just wanted to reassure her that Rex is okay. You know how she worries."

Although he says this nonchalantly, I tense up because I feel how hard he is working to normalize this conversation. Then I speak from inside a numb fog. "Where did they say the plane was headed?"

"Well, she thought they said it was coming from Tampa to Washington."

"Then that can't be it," I responded too quickly, adrenaline now starting to pump. We breathe.

Into the silence my brother says, "But there was confusion because they said it was Flight 90."

"That's his flight number, but Mom probably just got the number wrong." Yes, that's the explanation, I assure myself.

"No," he says, "I just heard the number myself on the radio."

"Did they say Air Florida?"

"I don't know, just that it had crashed into the Potomac."

"Oh, God. I'll call the airline and call you right back."

Flashes of lightning go off behind my eyes. My breathing speeds up, yet I am suffocating. As I dial, my hands shake, and I say aloud over and over, "No, please, God." Struck by the triviality of my everyday concerns, I remember how rushed I had felt getting ready for Rex's arrival and how important that had seemed. Now, if he is only alive, nothing else will matter. Of course he is, I admonish myself. Calm down. Mom has this all messed up. But then how did Art hear the same flight number?

I get a busy signal a couple of times before an Air Florida agent responds, "Air Florida, may I help you?"

The familiar greeting comforts me. See, there's nothing wrong, I reassure myself. "Yes, I want information on an arrival time."

"Certainly. What is the flight number?" he asks cheerfully.

"Flight 90."

Now his voice takes on a business-like quality as he quickly replies, "We cannot give out information on that flight."

"What do you mean you can't give out information on that flight?"

"We can't give out information on that flight," he repeats.

My heart pounds as I calmly ask, "Did an Air Florida plane crash today?"

"Yes."

"Was it going from Washington to Tampa?"

"Yes," he says, seeming relieved to answer my questions.

"How many flights do you have going from Washington to Tampa today?"

"Two."

"When were they scheduled?"

"One this morning. One this afternoon."

"Did the one this morning make it?"

"Yes."

"Thank you very much," I say softly and hang up the phone, my heart pounding.

Art answers on the first ring. "There was a crash," I say, "And it sounds like it was Rex's plane."

"They are saying now there are survivors," says my brother, and I feel hope. He continues, "I'm going to Mom and Dad's. They're pretty upset. They're going to be more upset."

"Okay, yes, go. We'll keep in touch."

Now I am alone, in shock, adrenaline rushing through my body. Numb on the outside, my insides are over-stimulated. I tumble through blank space. "Please, God, no," I hear myself moaning deeply from my gut. I move quickly to turn on the television. "Flight 90 crashes." It rings in my ears. "There are survivors in the water being rescued. Look another head." This is not a movie or an instant replay. I sit, my arms wrapped around my body, and sway back and forth twelve inches from the TV, breathing deeply and groaning. My eyes are glued to the rescue of the victims from the Potomac, and I search frantically for Rex. "He has to be there," I say out loud. In a daze, I am conscious of myself watching the TV as part of the scene. Reality becomes hazy, and more multi-layered and boundary-less than usual.

A car approaches and I know from the familiar sound that it is Gene, my partner, and Beth, his daughter, home from shopping. When I rush to the door, the fog lifts suddenly and the slow-motion scene I am in slips into fast-forward. "What's wrong, honey?" Gene asks as he steps through the door, drops his packages to the floor, and embraces me.

Quietly and desperately, I say, "My brother's plane crashed."

"Oh, my God," he says calmly. "Do something!" I want to yell. "Make it okay." But I say nothing. His body quivers; his embrace tightens. It feels good to be held and to have told someone. Not just someone. Gene, my anchor. He will know what to do and how to think about what has happened. My body slumps against his. "Oh, my God," he says again.

"It doesn't seem real," I say.

"Death never does," he replies. "But it is." Death? Why is he talking about death? It's just a crash. I cry quietly.

Then like a shot, I remember. "The TV. I've got to get back to the TV. There are survivors," and I break free from his embrace. That's right—he doesn't know there are survivors. That's why he's talking about death. "I'll see Rex being pulled from the river," I say loudly, fists clenched in the air. "Then I'll know he's all right. He had to make it. He's tough. There are survivors," I repeat.

Beth and Gene don't watch the instant replays of the people floundering in the icy water. Why do they sit silently at the kitchen table? They should be helping me look for Rex. They must not believe me. But they don't know him like I do. He can get himself out of anything. Any minute his head will appear. I continue rocking back and forth with my hands clasped together, periodically putting my face against the television screen to get a closer view. But I cannot find my brother in the Monet-like dots and lines. Hope and desperation alternate—hope when a new survivor is sighted, desperation when it is not Rex. There must be more survivors. "Rex, pop out of the fucking water!" I scream.

The announcers talk about the hero who just died saving others. "That must be Rex," I say, feeling proud. "He would do that. That's what he was like." Was? Why am I using the past tense? "He's not dead," I say. "I know he isn't." But if he has to be dead, I want him to be the hero. But then I will be angry that he could have saved himself and didn't. Why aren't Gene and Beth responding to me? They sit, silent, sad, watching me. He's not dead. Quit acting like he's dead. Of course he's not dead. Not my brother. I continue watching what are now the same instant replays of the same people being pulled out of the same river. Twelve people have survived. Then they announce seven. Then there are five. And one dead hero.

At my parents' home, the people came. Three to four hundred of them. They occupied my parents and validated for me how important Rex had been. I became the greeter, letting them in, hugging, listening to them marvel at how I had changed, and then directing them to my parents, who sat side-by-side in their matching Lazy-Boy chairs. Offering their sympathies, men looked sad and stoically held my father's hand and kissed my mother. Women were more likely to cry openly with my mother and often with my father, sometimes falling into sobs into my parents' arms. Older people comforted, while the younger ones stammered about not knowing what to say. That would come with experience. My mother cried continually and my father wiped tears constantly. I was the dry-eyed director, who craved and feared collapsing into my parents' embrace.

Everyone came bearing food. The smell was sickening. Knowing exactly what to do, several community women took over the kitchen. They served big meals to whoever was there, ignoring that no one ate much. Later in the week, it would take hours to throw away all the uneaten food: green beans cooked with hamhock; whole Old Virginia hams—the real ones, salty, strong, and fat; green and red Jell-O salads embedded with nuts and coconut, made in circular tins with globs of Miracle Whip filling the middle hole; apple pies made quickly from canned apples with dough crisscrossed on the top and too much cinnamon added; sweet pound cakes, chocolate layer cakes with chocolate icing, and yellow cakes with white frosting; big, fluffy white loaves of Wonder Bread; gallons of sweet tea in pickle jars that still tasted and smelled of pickles. Years later, I would find containers of instant coffee—the family size—and CoffeeMate and hundreds of plastic utensils still bundled in plastic wrappers in the cabinets.

Part of the role of greeter was to record who had brought what so that thank-you cards could be sent. My sister and I took turns keeping records. Sometimes I wanted to scream, "What a waste of time and energy!" Other times I was glad for the task and respected the final ritual of acknowledgement.

Mixed in with the mourners came the florists with the flowers we had requested not be sent. Donations for my parents' church also poured in. "What can we do?" everyone asked. "Write some thank-you notes," I wanted to say, but didn't. It was not their job. "Then go help throw food away," I thought, but again I said nothing. Proper etiquette dictated that you wait until people insisted—or better yet, just did something. I had never been involved in a funeral before, but I intuitively knew the rules. They were an extension of the small-town etiquette that I had lived the first twenty-two years of my life in.

I helped my mother make up a list of pallbearers. "They should be his best friends," she instructs. "It can't be relatives. They have to be men. There must be six." This is not the time to argue for women pallbearers. This is for my mother.

YOUR PROJECT: WRITING THE SELF

The excerpt from my autoethnography shared above shows how I reveal my innermost thoughts and feelings during an especially tragic and emotional moment—finding out that my brother has died in a plane crash. I take you into the immediacy of the moment. The first part of the story is told in the present. I invite you to be there with me as I hope for life and then come to the realization that my brother is dead. In the next segment, I take you into my parents' house, the day before the funeral. Now I am the greeter for those who come bearing food and sympathy. I tell this part of the story to you in the past, to provide some relief from the intense emotional immediacy of the first segment. In this second section, I become the observer, the ethnographer who shows you the small-town rituals of death and funerals, as I rediscover them for myself.

The story focuses on my emotional experience of my brother's death. In addition, this piece looks at the reaction to sudden death, media images of accidents, corporate response to tragedy, the juxtaposition of hope and facing reality, family communication in times of tragedy, and small-town responses and rituals surrounding death.

Keep the following points in mind as you carry out a similar project. First, think back to an event that was particularly emotional for you or think about one you are currently going through. Type out or write down all you can remember about the experience. Try to remember conversations that you had and reconstruct them as best you can to show how you are feeling. You may become emotional as you do so. Remember that you will not actually be in the experience and trust that you can bring yourself out of the emotionality whenever you need to. Continue writing for a few days. Your memories and feelings will stimulate other memories and feelings.

If possible, talk with others who are part of this episode and ask them what they remember. As you talk to and listen to them, you will remember other events. With their permission, record or write down these stories. Make sure to secure the permission of other characters you include, if possible. If not, think deeply about the ethical implications of writing about those who have not given permission and do not know you are including their stories in your story.

Finally, read through all your notes and think about how you want to tell this story. It is important to figure out which part of the story you want to tell, since you can't tell everything. It is important that the story be evocative and engaging, inviting readers to enter the story or to think about their own.

Using your notes, write your story. Be sure to include vivid descriptions of the scene and of your thoughts and feelings. Use dialogue. This is the time to try to look at the story from outside the experience. Think about your writing. Think about what the story means. Think about what a reader can learn from the story, in addition to finding out about your experience. What social processes are revealed in your story? Make sure you develop them, but do so narratively. The emphasis should be on *showing*, not *telling*.

Reread your story and share it with others for feedback. Take that feedback into consideration in preparing a final draft, and write a conclusion that analyzes the story and discusses what can be learned from it. With your instructor's approval, consider reading the story aloud to the class.

Messianic Judaism: Searching the Spirit
by Leigh Berger

I stand with my head bowed during a worship service at Dalet Shalom Messianic Jewish Congregation, thinking about my ethnography and the two years I have spent with these congregants. Messianic Jews identify themselves as Jewish, carrying out Jewish rituals and celebrations within the context of a belief in Jesus (Yeshua). Messianic Jews are not accepted by mainstream Jews because of their insistence that Yeshua is the Messiah; they have a conflicted relationship with mainstream Christians because they believe that Christianity's understanding of the Bible is misguided. Simultaneously defining themselves as Jewish while believing in Yeshua places Messianic Jews in an undefined borderland. I am fascinated by this boundary existence, in part because I can understand being frustrated with mainstream Judaism and desiring a highly emotional practice of religion.

My thoughts turn to my own ambivalence about being Jewish, and I wonder how much of that feeling is rooted in the context of my familial history. I always felt like I was born with a mark of shame on my soul. As though deep within me—already present at conception—was a reminder of faces and bodies pressed tightly into train compartments headed for Auschwitz. As though the genetic mass within my mother's womb, dividing and subdividing, already felt the twinges of comprehension that, from that moment on, Judaism would become a constant reminder of victimhood.

What do my memories of life with my parents tell me? I am half of their union. Half of my father, half of my mother. I am half of both their happiness and sadness. Half of each of their minimal Jewish loyalty. As a family we marked our Jewish identity three times a year: Yom Kippur, Hanukkah, and Passover.

And now I am surrounded by people worshiping in an evangelical style, but with loyalty to Jewish identity and ritual. The congregants at Dalet Shalom express their Jewishness with passion and emotion, but within the context of belief in Yeshua, the figure not accepted as the Messiah by mainstream Jews.

I am pulled out of my internal reflection by the voice of Dalet Shalom's rabbi, Aaron Levinson. "Just relax and receive the Lord. Don't try and fight it, just receive." A quiet melody swirls around us, and I slowly sway back and forth. "Open your heart and receive the Lord. Anyone who hasn't yet received Yeshua, but who would like to now open your heart to him, please come forward." There is a pause, and I open my eyes, wondering if this invitation is directed toward me. I think I am the only person there who hasn't accepted Yeshua as their savior. Suspended in the interval, I am uncomfortable with my own resistance, wishing a deep spiritual experience could move me into complete belonging. Since much of my interpretation is shaped by my role as semi-participant, I wonder if conversion would allow me full participation, thereby profoundly altering the ethnography that I write.

"Rabbi! Rabbi! I had a vision!" shouts a woman to my right. "I've been questioning my belief and what I should do, but today I had a vision. There was a man in a white robe, sitting on a throne. And as I came closer, I sensed two more people on either side of him, also in white. I felt them all reach out for me, and it was so peaceful. Just peace. And I knew that it was the Messiah."

"Amen!" congregants call out while clapping.

"Hallelujah!" others yell.

I close my eyes again. What would it be like to "receive" the Lord? I turn this thought over in my mind and begin to imagine a white-robed Jesus, looking much like he does in millions of artistic renderings. I imagine his hand reaching toward me, reaching and waiting for my acceptance. I try to imagine my own salvation: what would happen if my own hand reached back to Him? Would the hand be inviting? Would I feel safe, secure, and unburdened?

I know I have a deep desire for spiritual fulfillment. The urge for it has always filled me like a hunger, causing me to seek it out continually, but without complete satisfaction. At Dalet Shalom, I love the feeling of joining in praise and worship, of having Rabbi Levinson ask about my emotional well-being, of how it feels when congregants invite me to sit with them during services. However, I feel estranged by their belief in biblical literalism, by their intolerance of homosexuality, and by their insistence that there is only one correct way to worship. Because of those disconnections I wonder if it would ever be possible to convert to Messianic Judaism. I want the intense emotional energy of Dalet Shalom and the warmth and caring among members. I want the moments of transcendence offered by the singing and dancing and the link to the sights and sounds of my heritage.

Toward the end of the service, Rabbi Levinson asks us to repeat a prayer, but offers a condition: "Please do not repeat the prayer if you have not recognized Yeshua. It is very important to only say these words if you believe in Yeshua, because it is a contract with the Lord! It is urgent that you decide to live in light rather than walk on a dark path to Hell." He begins the prayer.

I remain silent. But a moment later I am reconnected when Rabbi Levinson covers his head with his *tallit* and performs the Aaronic benediction in Hebrew *a capella*. "May the Lord bless thee and keep thee. May the Lord cause his countenance to shine upon thee . . ." This ritual strikes me deep within my soul, the Hebrew words gliding over the familiar melody, binding me in a breathtaking moment to the generation that came before me.

That night, I have a dream about my grandfather. After his death seven years ago, he would frequently appear in my dreams, but I have not dreamed of him in many years. He is standing in the kitchen of the south Florida condo where he and my grandmother lived for most of my life. I enter the room and he smiles warmly at me. His startlingly blue eyes light up, and he brushes some of his soft white hair away from his forehead.

"Grandpa?" Contrary to real life, in the dream I feel like I am physically much smaller than he and I have an impression of him towering over me.

He continues to smile at me, and somehow I know that he is leaving to walk to synagogue, like he does every Friday. Both he and my grandmother were religious Jews who attended synagogue regularly and followed the Jewish dietary laws of keeping *kosher*. My grandfather holds up a hand, as though waving good-bye to me.

"Grandpa? I need to ask you . . ."

But he is slowly turning away from me, until I can no longer see his face. I desperately want him to turn back around, to answer my questions. I awake from the dream with a start, confused for a moment about where I am and what has happened. I realize that I have been dreaming and I smile at the memory of my grandfather. "I miss you," I whisper into the dark room and close my eyes again.

I have had this dream because of my research, because he and my grandmother were observant Jews, and because I have been questioning my own religious beliefs. I wonder if my grandfather's turning away symbolizes my feeling that I have rejected part of my Jewish identity. After all, I am not an observant Jew, and now I'm studying a congregation of people who are considered traitors among the majority of Jewish Americans. What would I have asked my grandfather if I hadn't lost his attention? What was the comfort he got out of his faith? What was his conception of God? Maybe his overlooking my questions symbolized how difficult they are to answer. Maybe he was trying to tell me that not all questions *can* be answered.

Memories and dreams such as this continue to surface during my fieldwork, ghosts of my past woken up by my insistent probing. The more I travel into the Messianic world, the more I realize I have embarked upon a parallel journey of self-exploration.

YOUR PROJECT: WRITING THE SELF AND OTHERS

The portion of my ethnography shared above shows how I both describe Dalet Shalom and simultaneously reveal my own internal feelings and memories. I connect my discoveries of Dalet Shalom to my own life and experiences, using myself as a vehicle for exploring Messianic Judaism. Since we have no way to systematically examine concepts like God or the afterlife, we must study them by looking at how people talk about and describe their religious experiences to themselves and others. I open religious belief by showing the interactions between the lives of my participants and my own accounts of my life and experiences as a Jewish woman. Keep the following points in mind as you carry out a similar project.

Choose a religious congregation or other formal gathering that you wish to observe. It can be either one that is new to you or one with which you have some personal experience. Find out times of services and/or gatherings and meetings. Call the group and be prepared to explain that you are observing as part of a class assignment. If they will only welcome you if you promise to become a full-fledged member, respect their position, but find another group to study. In any case, make sure you have permission to observe (it will be useful to have it in writing, particularly if your school requires you to file a formal informed consent application) and then plan to attend at least two of the meetings.

Take a notepad with you when you go to the service/meeting unless you have explicit permission to use either audio- or videotape. Try not to spend the entire meeting, however, taking notes. It is better to write down your descriptions, feelings, and reactions immediately after the meeting. Some questions you might want to ask yourself include: How/why did you choose this particular group to observe? How did you feel emotionally during the service/meeting? Why do you think you felt this way? Did you understand what was going on? Why or why not? How do the activities at this meeting compare with others that you have observed or participated in? Is this a group you could become part of? Why or why not?

Look over your notes and put together a narrative account of your observations (both of the group and its meetings and about your own reactions). The narrative should have a clear beginning (in which you set up your history with this topic, your decision to choose this group, and a basic description of who they are and where they are located), a middle (in which you describe the scene, people, and activities), and conclusion. In the conclusion, reflect on whether or not you could be a member of this group. Explain why or why not. If you have selected a group of which you are already a member, explore whether or not playing the role of observer made you more or less committed to the group. What did you learn about ethnography? What did you learn about your own emotions and perceptions?

16

Participating in an Ethnographic Field School

James M. Tim Wallace

As you have learned, the ability to carry out ethnographic research, one of the hallmarks of professional anthropology and other social sciences, consists of a set of skills that even beginning students can master. Ethnographic research skills can be effectively utilized in many settings outside of traditional communities, including business, education, and health care. It is with good reason, then, that all undergraduate and graduate programs in anthropology (and an increasing number of programs in other fields) require coursework in ethnographic methods. Most methods courses require some hands-on experience, but there are obvious limitations imposed by other demands on students' time. So if you really want to find out what ethnography is all about and how to do it, it is a good idea to attend an ethnographic field school, which will give you time to focus your attention on a single set of learning activities without the interference of other coursework assignments.

WHAT IS AN ETHNOGRAPHIC FIELD SCHOOL?

As I use the term, "ethnographic field school" means an intensive, extended stay in a locale significantly different from the student's usual surroundings, during which time the program's director combines instruction in ethnographic methods with the conduct of an actual research project. That project may be either independently conceived and carried out by each student under the supervision of the director, or it may be a group project with all the students contributing to a common final product. In some cases, the students' research will be integrated into the director's ongoing research in the area in which the school is held. Ethnographic field schools all require students to practice taking organized field notes and/or keeping formal field journals and to submit these documents along with the actual product(s) of research. Field schools also give some form of university credit; the normal load is six credits for a four-to-six week program.

Beyond these basics, however, there is considerable variation in what field schools have to offer. Variation is due to differences inherent in the research settings, the theoretical interests of the program director, the educational backgrounds of the student participants, and the degree to which other languages must be learned. Some schools have structured activities involving frequent contact with the participants, while others are more loosely structured and expect that students will be able to work independently most of the time. Most field schools have some kind of home-stay component; in some cases, it may be merely a brief overnighter, with students living mainly in dormitories, hotels, or community buildings; but in other cases, the student may board with a local family for the duration of the school. Some programs last for an entire academic semester while others last for a few weeks (usually during the summer).

There are other kinds of field schools that can be interesting and valuable to anthropology and other students. For example, there are archaeology field schools in which students assist the project director in excavating and analyzing a dig. There are field schools that are essentially guided study tours of famous or important heritage or ethnic sites in which the program leader is mainly a lecturer to students in a mobile classroom. There are still other field schools whose purpose is mainly language study. But my remarks in this chapter are directed mainly toward an understanding of the true ethnographic field school as described above.

LEARNING OBJECTIVES OF
ETHNOGRAPHIC FIELD SCHOOLS

All ethnographic-field-school programs try to provide opportunities for a student to learn ethnographic research skills, to learn something about the culture of the community under study, and—perhaps most important—to internalize the psychological "right stuff" one needs to do the job of an ethnographer. In a real sense, field schools give a student the opportunity to be an apprentice ethnographer.

There are some concrete skills that are part of the learning package. I emphasize the following skills in my own six-week ethnographic field school in Costa Rica: designing a field research project; selecting appropriate research methods or data-collection techniques based on a realistic appraisal of the field site; defining and utilizing appropriate sampling procedures; developing daily and weekly research goals; writing field notes and keeping a journal; coding field notes; carrying out systematic observation techniques; understanding ethical issues involved in fieldwork; conducting both formal and informal interviews; working effectively with informants and translators; developing appropriate rapport-building devices; carrying out community and cognitive mapping; understanding how and when to use rapid appraisal techniques; understanding time-allocation study techniques; surviving and overcoming culture shock; using laptop computers for simple research tasks; analyzing ethnographic data; and writing effective research reports.

It is very important for students to become competent participants in the local culture. Participation opens them to listening and observing the culture in which they find themselves—a key skill to develop in ethnographic research—so they can build rapport, gain the confidence of the local people, know what kinds of questions to ask, and of whom to ask them.

By way of preparation, it is usually a good idea to have taken a course or read books and articles about the culture you will be visiting and working in. Most students in my program will have done some background reading and other library research before arriving in the field so they can hit the ground running as soon as they enter the site. Since the program lasts only six weeks, it is important that they have some knowledge and understanding before they get to the school. Some field schools in fact build specific ethnographic, topical, or language courses into their orientation programs.

TWO EXAMPLES OF ETHNOGRAPHIC FIELD SCHOOLS

My field school is an intensive six-week summer training program in Costa Rica in which students from my own university (North Carolina State University) and other universities around the U.S. and the world gather to learn what ethnographic field research is all about and how to undertake their own independent fieldwork. I have had applications from students in Asia, Africa, Europe, and North and South America. In 2000 one of the participants was a student working toward an M.A. in anthropology from the University of Edinburgh, Scotland. In 1999 one of the students was an undergraduate from a university in Medellín, Colombia, and another was a graduate student from Japan. Since my first field school in 1994, over 100 students have participated. I have also led workshops for professional colleagues interested in organizing ethnographic field schools of their own. Often students from colleagues' universities participate in my program, and sometimes my students participate in theirs. We encourage our students to find the program that best fits their academic and intellectual needs and interests.

There is a maximum of fifteen students for each session of my field school. The first third of the program consists of formal classes, fieldwork exercises, and informal discussion sessions. By the end of the second week, all students have selected a topic, written a research project outline, and begun their ethnographic data collection. By the end of the program, each student will have completed an independent project. A fifteen-page preliminary written report must be completed before departure.

Throughout the program each student lives with a local family, which I consider to be a vital component in their training. My students consistently tell me in their program evaluations that the home-stay was the single most valuable aspect of the program. The home-stay is not simply a place to sleep and eat. The families have been carefully chosen ahead of time for their interest in and enthusiasm for providing the students with a safe, friendly environment for learning about the community. The families are as excited about having the students stay in their homes as the students are to find out what the local people's real home life is like. The families are their first key informants and collaborators who help them get the most out of their ethnographic experience. Many of the families are quite interested in the students' research and are even anxious to help them in their work. Students are able to depart with an appreciation of what it takes to do ethnographic fieldwork, not only because of what they have learned in the classroom, but also from their experience of doing fieldwork on their own. Collaboration with their home-stay families helps them get involved quickly and intensively with the local community so they can do their independent project. In the long run, what the students learn experientially on their own has more lasting value than what they learn in class.

Another field school takes place in Barbados and is directed by George and Sharon Gmelch of Union College in Schenectady, New York. Their program, however, is three months long and offered in alternate years, instead of six weeks and annually like mine. All the Barbados program students are from Union College. The program is well known on campus, students are easily recruited by word-of-mouth, and former participants play a key role in the recruitment and orientation of new students. Nearly all the students are anthropology majors and have had several appropriate courses in preparation for their experience abroad. In addition, in the semester prior to departure, the selected participants are required to sign up for on-campus orientation sessions, read books on the Caribbean and related topics from a prepared bibliography, and interact with former field-school students. All the students are undergraduates, and the total group of participants is relatively small, so students have frequent one-on-one access to the program directors. Because the Barbados project lasts for three months, it is possible for participants to build strong relationships with their research subjects. They can develop more detailed projects, deal with culture shock, and develop a high level of competency in ethnographic data-collection skills. Moreover, since English is the language of Barbados, it is possible for the students to begin interacting with local people immediately.

A week-long on-site orientation in Barbados includes some classroom work on ethnographic methods (including detailed discussion of writing field notes) and the completion of some warm-up ethnographic fieldwork exercises. After this orientation, the students are assigned to their home-stay families. The students live in separate communities spread around the island, and each one completes an independent research project. Each student must submit a preliminary report before departure. During the three months, the directors visit each student in his or her community at least once a week. The students rarely interact with each other, except on weekends; most of their week is taken up with their own projects. The directors expect the students to make themselves and their purpose known to members of the community, to develop a network of acquaintances and friends, and to become integrated as much as possible into the life of the community. Although the directors are always available to mentor the students, the latter are expected to test their own ethnographic wings and work on their own as much as they can.

ADVANTAGES OF PARTICIPATING IN A FIELD SCHOOL

The presence of an on-site program director is a real asset to the participants. A good field-school program director is one who is more a mentor than a teacher. In the long run, the only way to learn ethnographic methods is to do actual ethnographic research. A teacher can never do the learning for you, but a mentor can be there for you when you need a word of encouragement, advice about handling a sensitive subject, a suggestion about how to work with a difficult informant, an idea about how to organize one's data for the write-up, or tips on coping with culture shock.

The director/mentor can play a decisive role in helping students understand that culture shock is a natural part of the learning process. No matter how familiar the setting may be, the immersion into the local culture that is required in an extended piece of ethnographic research can be an unsettling experience, and when it hits students can be confused and upset—perhaps even ashamed that they are doing something wrong. The mentor helps them handle the shock of living in a new setting and plays a key role in getting them back to normal. For example, a few years ago one of my field-school students spent about $1000 in telephone calls to an intimate friend back home. I suspected that this student was trying to cope with severe culture shock. Rather than criticize the student's costly coping strategy, I decided to change the home-stay to a more nurturing family. As a result, the student felt more comfortable in the community and more confident in conducting the research. After graduation, this student told me that the field school had been the most important and meaningful aspect of the entire four college years. In general, the positive experience of completing an interesting and useful research product convinces students that culture shock, while distressing, need not be fatal. Having a mentor around makes it a bit easier to find out that they have the "right stuff" to be an ethnographer after all.

STUDENT COMMENTS ABOUT THE LONG-TERM VALUE OF A FIELD SCHOOL

In addition to the concrete skills students develop as participants in field schools, there are also positive, long-term outcomes (such as learning how to cope with culture shock) that are just as important, even if they are intangible, personal, and sometimes difficult to describe. For example, one undergraduate wrote me about the impact of the Costa Rica field school:

> I had traveled a lot in the military, but I was scared when you dropped me off with my host family that first rainy night when we arrived. . . . Going to Costa Rica reminded me that there is a world out there. I think about people from where I live who have no conception of different places. They live in their reality and there is no other for them. I guess the field school experience has made me want to remain outside a small cultural bubble. I wish sometimes I was a millionaire so I could go on a field study somewhere different every year.

Another undergraduate wrote:

> I have become much more culturally sensitive since the trip, and I feel as though I understand much more the importance of and need for diversity throughout the world. My research at [Manuel Antonio National Park in Costa Rica] secured my decision to pursue environmental education and awareness, and because of the trip I am planning to live outside the U.S. at some point for an extended period of time, hopefully to study environmental awareness and protection. Living within a different culture, although brief, helped me to surface and develop many of the passions and interests that I needed to grow on a personal level. I discovered both positive and negative aspects of myself and my ability to relate to other people, which helped me to focus on personal improvement and identification.

A final example comes from another undergraduate who wrote me to say:

> Amazingly enough, I believe that I experienced a hefty dose of culture shock coming home from Costa Rica. I had a hard time easing back into air-conditioning and hot showers once I realized they were truly luxuries! The field school taught me so much about the world, and quite unexpectedly, about myself. Quite honestly, I don't think that my family and friends knew how to react to the new, wiser, and more anthropologically confident me. Working in the field gave me a greater appreciation for what classroom learning provided, and motivated me to continue my interests in tourism. The program made me more aware of other people and places. It gave me the capabilities to bridge different perspectives to foster greater understanding and positive change.

ANOTHER PRACTICAL REASON FOR A FIELD SCHOOL

There is also a good financial reason to participate in an ethnographic field school. It is a good place to find out whether you are psychologically suited to be an anthropologist. If, by the end of the program, it turns out you are not so inclined, you will save lots of money and time studying anthropology as an undergraduate major or in a graduate program. The field school gives you an opportunity to find out what ethnographic fieldwork is really like. Not all students end up convinced they should stay in anthropology and make a career of conducting ethnographic research. One very good student switched her major to journalism shortly after returning to campus. She had done well in the field, but decided that anthropology was not the best match for her talents. She was neither the first, nor will she be the last, anthropology major to change programs after attending a field school.

Students are understandably anxious about their dedication to and skill in cultural anthropology, but having doubts about one's ability to do fieldwork are not at all uncommon. In a book entitled *Fieldnotes*, anthropologist

Roger Sanjek presents evidence of how even the most famous ethnographers experienced such doubts; in their private notes, they wondered why they were in the field at all. Michael Agar, author of *The Professional Stranger*, expressed the same fears about his own fieldwork. I, too, was terrified of doing my dissertation research and got angry with my professors because I thought they had not trained me well enough. I thought I had learned precious little about how to do such basic tasks as writing field notes, interviewing, taking genealogies, analyzing coded data, mapping, and taking censuses. Fieldwork is a challenge that can be overwhelming if one has to face it alone for the first time. I therefore decided to organize a field school that would be open to both beginning students as well as to graduate students on the threshold of their own independent research.

I have learned in my years of directing a field school that students feel more comfortable testing their wings when they know that someone with experience is available for advice and guidance. Fear of rejection and fear of failure are two normal emotions that both apprentice and professional ethnographers confront when they enter the field to do research. But in a field school, these fears can be assuaged in a reasonably comfortable, supportive atmosphere. In this kind of program, students not only have a mentor available when a problem arises (or even when it is only anticipated)—they can also find support and encouragement from other participants who are going through the same process of adjustment and learning.

In the end, though, doing ethnographic fieldwork is fun, and when it all comes together in an interesting and useful product, it can be exhilarating. In the field school you can share both your failures and your successes with everyone else in the program. When you get home you will find you have been changed for the better, even if the changes are invisible to all but you and those closest to you (including, perhaps, your professors). The other people who attended field school with you, however, will understand what has happened to you, since they shared that time and had similar feelings. You will never forget the people with whom you went into the field, for they have shared with you a very important moment in your life—the moment when you became a real ethnographer.

SOME CONCLUDING ADVICE

By participating in an ethnographic field school, undergraduates can see what kinds of skills are needed to be an anthropologist. Graduate students can also benefit by gaining hands-on experience prior to undertaking their own independent thesis or dissertation research projects. Even post-doctoral professionals can participate in these programs as refreshers or as a way to learn new and innovative techniques. What unites all students who participate in an ethnographic field school is the opportunity to test themselves in a cross-cultural setting under the tutelage of an experienced mentor who provides structure and lots of encouragement and support when the going gets tough. The mentor-student interaction process is a vital component of all ethnographic field schools and is an important reason for their popularity.

If you are interested in the possibility of joining a field school, the first place to look is your own university. If it does not have a program of its own, it may be able to help you locate programs elsewhere; in some cases, financial support may be available for students wishing to participate in such a program. Another good source of information is *Anthropology News*, the monthly (except June, July, and August) newsletter of the American Anthropological Association, which has a "Career Development" section in which field-school opportunities are announced. You can also contact the AAA directly and request information from the program assistant in charge of keeping a list of field-school programs. The AAA office is located at 4350 N. Fairfax Drive, Suite 640, Arlington, VA 22203-1620; the phone number is 703-528-1902, and the website is at http://www.aaanet.org. The newsletter of the Society for Applied Anthropology also regularly publishes field-school information. Announcements also appear on various anthropology listservs. Ask your instructor which ones he or she thinks are most appropriate for you to monitor, or ask him or her to keep track of some of them for you.

When you identify a program that interests you, it is essential that you speak in person to the program director. Since s/he will be the main person you will be dealing with in the field, be sure to interview him or her in as much detail as possible; find out about how the program is structured, how much mentoring you will receive, whether a home-stay is part of the program, how many credits you will be earning, what kind of product you will be responsible for submitting, and how much access you will have to the director. Be sure also to clarify all logistical matters: all costs (including airfare), insurance, inoculations (if needed), and passport and visa requirements. Do not be afraid to ask for as many details as you think you need to make an informed decision. On the basis of all this information, you can make a reasonable decision about whether the program suits your needs and interests. If you want further suggestions, advice, or information, you may also contact me at tim_wallace@ncsu.edu. I also have a website at http://www4.ncsu.edu/~twallace.

A FEW SELECTED REFERENCES FOR FURTHER INFORMATION

Agar, Michael. 1996. *The Professional Stranger: An Informal Introduction to Ethnography*, 2nd ed. San Diego: Academic Press.

Gmelch, George, and Sharon B. Gmelch. 1999. An Ethnographic Field School: What Students Do and Learn. *Anthropology and Education Quarterly* 30(2):220–227.

Sanjek, Roger, ed. 1990. *Fieldnotes: The Makings of Anthropology.* New York: Cornell University Press.

Wallace, James M. Tim. 1999. Introduction: Mentoring Apprentice Ethnographers through Field Schools. *Anthropology and Education Quarterly* 30(2):210–219.

Contributors

Michael V. Angrosino is Professor of Anthropology at the University of South Florida where he teaches courses in cultural anthropology, applied anthropology, anthropological theory, oral history, and comparative religion. He was the founding director of the University Honors Program and has served as Editor of *Human Organization*, the journal of the Society for Applied Anthropology. His publications include *Field Projects in Anthropology: A Student Handbook* (with Julia Crane) and *Opportunity House: Ethnographic Stories of Mental Retardation*. His current projects include the analysis of life histories of adults with chronic mental illness and mental retardation and the development of workshops on cultural diversity for a variety of civic groups.

Yvette Baber is affiliated with the Anchin Center of the College of Education, University of South Florida.

Roberta D. Baer is Professor of Anthropology at the University of South Florida. Her research interests include medical and nutritional anthropology in Mexican and Mexican-American populations.

Jessica Barber is a candidate for the M.A. degree in applied anthropology at the University of South Florida.

Leigh Berger loves to observe and write about the world around her. She especially enjoys encouraging her students at Shoreline Community College to write about and share their own experiences as a way to discover how things they learn in the classroom connect to their lives. When not writing or teaching, she can be found playing fetch with her puppy, traveling with Jonathan, her partner, cooking, and enjoying the time she spends with her friends. She is currently working on publishing a book about her experiences in the Messianic Jewish community.

S. Elizabeth Bird is Professor of Anthropology at the University of South Florida. She has published widely in the field of cultural studies and media.

Kathryn Borman is Professor of Anthropology and Associate Director of the Anchin Center of the College of Education at the University of South Florida. She specializes in the study of educational issues, particularly in urban contexts.

Constance P. DeRoche went to Nova Scotia to do the fieldwork on which this chapter is based and has been teaching there, at the University College of Cape Breton, ever since. Her more recent research includes work on media stereotypes, organizational culture and change, and community economic development. She has taught courses on societal problems, the use and abuse of biology, work, and organizational culture. She particularly enjoys designing hands-on course projects.

Carolyn Ellis loves to write stories, experiment with form, think about social-science methods, and feel and consider emotional experience. She enjoys teaching and writing as a Professor of Communication and Sociology at the University of South Florida. When she's not working, she can be found lifting weights, traveling or making plans to travel, walking in the woods, engaging in and observing herself in intense relational conversations, or playing unselfconsciously with her partner Art Bochner and their four dogs. Especially happy to have written *Final Negotiations* and edited *Composing Ethnography* as well as *Ethnographically Speaking* (both with Art Bochner), she will be happier still when she completes *Doing Autoethnography: A Methodological Novel*.

Bill Goddard is a graduate student in applied anthropology at the University of South Florida.

Guy Hagen received his bachelor's degree in anthropology and computer science from the University of Minnesota and his master's degree in applied urban anthropology from the University of South Florida. He is currently the Assistant Director for Economic Development at the University of South Florida, where he is responsible for conducting economic and workforce research for regional development. He has published internationally on applied network, economic, and organization studies. His present research interests include computer networks and regional knowledge networks.

Amy Fox McNulty is a graduate student in applied anthropology at the University of South Florida.

Serena Nanda is Professor Emerita of Anthropology at John Jay College of Criminal Justice, City University of New York. She writes widely on gender, India, and the teaching of anthropology. Her published works include *Neither Man Nor Woman: The Hijras of India, American Cultural Pluralism,* and *Gender Diversity: Crosscultural Variations.* She is currently working on a book on art and ethnic identity.

V. Richard Persico, Jr. is Professor of Anthropology at Georgia Southern University where he is the coordinator of the undergraduate major in anthropology. His major research interests are the impact of rural-to-urban migration on community organization in the U.S. and Latin America and the ethnohistory of Native America. In 1998 he received the Georgia Southern University Award for Excellence in Instruction.

Laurie K. Price is a member of the faculty of California State University, Hayward. She is a medical anthropologist with a particular interest in health policy in Latin America and the United States.

Ellen Puccia is a graduate student in applied anthropology at the University of South Florida.

Nancy Redfern-Vance graduated from the University of Michigan in 1967 with a bachelor's degree in nursing and a minor in psychology. She attended a nurse-midwifery program at the University of Mississippi Medical School and was certified as a nurse-midwife in 1975. During her midwifery career, she assisted more than 1400 mothers in the delivery of their babies. In 1993 she returned to graduate school and earned her master's degree in nursing administration from the University of Florida. She completed her doctorate in applied anthropology at the University of South Florida in 1999. Her research interests and publications revolve around women's health, women's policy issues, and program evaluation. She is now working as Director of Research in the Office of Performance Improvement at the Florida Department of Health.

Martha W. Rees is a member of the faculty of Agnes Scott College in Decatur, Georgia. She is a social anthropologist specializing in household economics in Mexico and among Mexican immigrants in the U.S. She has conducted research in Mexico for over fifteen years with support from the National Science Foundation and a Fulbright lectureship. Her chapter was written with the support of a Fulbright lectureship and the Centro de Investigación y Estudios Superiores en Antropología Social in Oaxaca, Mexico.

Cheryl Rodriguez is a faculty member in the Department of Africana Studies at the University of South Florida. She specializes in studies of women of color, microenterprise, and social welfare policies.

J. Jerome Smith is Associate Professor of Anthropology at the University of South Florida. A linguistic anthropologist, he has published on such topics as land tenure, dispute settlement, and conversational turn taking, always with a focus on the role of culture as an information-processing system facilitating human social interaction. His other major professional commitment has been to the development of instructional aids in the teaching of anthropology to undergraduates, such as software for kinship and lexicostatistical analysis. His most recent work has been in distance learning, combining text, telecourse, and Internet resources to create an award-winning self-paced introductory course in cultural anthropology.

Gerry Tierney is Associate Professor of Anthropology at Webster University, where she teaches Introduction to Cultural Anthropology, Culture and Communication, Cross-cultural Perspectives on Women, Women in the Criminal Justice System, and Applied Anthropology. She has taught in Webster University's overseas programs in Austria, Japan, and Thailand. Her most recent article, "Serendipity in the Field: Discovering Culture in Unexpected Places," discusses the qualitative research methods she used while in Japan. She is currently working on the life history of Araguchi Kochino, her neighbor and friend during the year in which she conducted research and taught at Asahikawa University, Hokkaido, Japan.

James M. Tim Wallace is Associate Professor of Sociology and Anthropology at North Carolina State University. With a focus on the anthropology of sustainable tourism, he has been leading ethnographic field schools in Hungary and Costa Rica since 1994.

Susan C. Weller is Professor of Preventive Medicine and Community Health and also of Family Medicine at the University of Texas Health Sciences Branch in Galveston. Her research interests include consensus analysis, cross-cultural comparisons, and health of Latino populations.

Alvin W. Wolfe is Distinguished Professor of Anthropology and Coordinator of Internships in Applied Anthropology at the University of South Florida. For more than twenty years he has directed the Human Services Information System, a database management system that uses up-to-date technology to help applied-anthropology interns keep up with ever-changing local information. He applies formal network analysis to many social situations, including a study of 600 organizations in the Tampa Bay area that serve children and families. He recently led a team in the study of welfare reform in Florida. He is chair of the Florida Health and Human Services Board.